Ideas for the Animated Short

Ideas for the Animated Short
Finding and Building Stories

Karen Sullivan, Gary Schumer, and Kate Alexander

ELSEVIER

AMSTERDAM • BOSTON • HEIDELBERG • LONDON
NEW YORK • OXFORD • PARIS • SAN DIEGO
SAN FRANCISCO • SINGAPORE • SYDNEY • TOKYO

Focal Press is an imprint of Elsevier

Focal Press

Associate Acquisitions Editor: Georgia Kennedy
Publishing Services Manager: George Morrison
Project Managers: Lianne Hong, Kathryn Liston
Editorial Assistant: Chris Simpson
Marketing Manager: Marcel Koppes
Cover Design: Fred Rose

Focal Press is an imprint of Elsevier
30 Corporate Drive, Suite 400, Burlington, MA 01803, USA
Linacre House, Jordan Hill, Oxford OX2 8DP, UK

Library of Congress Cataloging-in-Publication Data
Application submitted

British Library Cataloguing-in-Publication Data
A catalogue record for this book is available from the British Library.

ISBN: 978-0-240-80860-4

For information on all Focal Press publications
visit our website at www.books.elsevier.com

11 12   10 9 8 7 6 5

Printed in the United States of America.

Contents

Foreword

MEMO
To: Animated Short Film Directors
From: John Tarnoff, Head of Show Development, DreamWorks Animation

Short films aren't so different from feature films. The rules of storytelling still apply. But the beauty of short films is their ability to distill, in just a few minutes, the essence of an idea, and concentrate that essence in such a way that the audience is moved and stimulated in as strong a fashion as if they had just sat through a full-length feature film.

Animated short films provide even more opportunity to engage the viewer. Animated films are distinguished by the uniqueness of their artwork, and this completely invented and imagined aspect is what sets animated shorts so resolutely apart from live-action shorts. This is your challenge and your opportunity in the realm of animation—a realm where it takes both a graphical, painterly talent (and skill), in addition to a photographic, cinematic, and narrative inspiration. Because an animated film has so many more visual possibilities than a live-action film, the bar is significantly raised for the animation filmmaker to attempt something truly integral and affecting.

What makes for a good idea for a short animated film?

To fulfill their inspiration, filmmakers have many options to express the one idea. Just as mash-up videos show how it is possible to create different stories, genres, and styles out of existing material, at the concept stage in developing a short, filmmakers need to balance their inspiration with a format that, to their mind, best expresses the impact they want to make with their film.

This can mean that the film is narrative or non-narrative (poetic), that it draws from a particular artistic style, uses a particular style of animation, mixes up styles and genres to create something unique . . . the possibilities are endless.

While there are rules of good artistic composition, good storytelling, good character development, good visual design, and all of the large and small elements that go into the creation of a film, the filmmaker must not get bogged down by too many conventions that can be creatively stifling.

Animated films are films first and foremost. Films exist in five dimensions: the two dimensions of line, tone and color, the third dimension of space, the fourth dimension of time, and the fifth dimension of content. It is this fifth dimension that unites and binds the other four and, if successful, touches an audience and resonates with them in a mental, physical, emotional and artistic (some might say "spiritual") way.

How should fledgling filmmakers proceed? Assuming they have learned the basics and spent time cultivating their eye, their techniques, their tools, and most of all, their own creative voice, there are a few guidelines for jumping in. For me, a good film is always an exercise in contrasts and in the unexpected: a conventional story with unconventional characters or situations or, conversely, an unconventional story with a conventional character. It can be a conventional story with a surprising punch line, or maybe an unconventional, non-linear story that concludes in a familiar way. The point is to create a particular definitive and definable dynamic. Perhaps the film displays a specific, evolving color palette as it unfolds, and that palette reflects the precise evolution of the story or characters as they transform over the course of the narrative.

It is the dynamic (or dynamics) that supports the execution of the film and makes it intriguing beyond merely one's inspiration that it "seems like a good idea."

For the two-dimensional elements, there are centuries of artistic reference and a whole world of physical reference for artists to create the look of their film. Care should be taken to draw from multiple sources in synthesizing a single vision and to weigh those sources in comparison with one another. The filmmaker uses references, to build the look of the film and can create sketches or workbooks of ideas based on these references. This Visual Development phase is key, no matter what the size of the film is, as it must co-exist with the story in a highly compatible way for the film to work. Various design elements assist the filmmaker in creating a visual script for the ultimate look of the film. Set designs, whether in rough line sketches or fully rendered paintings, establish the locations or environments where the film will take place. Color and lighting keys establish the flow of visual elements over the course of the film. Character designs and turnarounds establish the look of the characters and their visual relationships to one another. While a short animated film is arguably less complex than a full-length feature, because it is short, it is subject to perhaps increased scrutiny or attention as all of its design elements will be so much more important in proportion to the length of the overall film. People will look more closely at a short film, and expect more from it, merely because it is expected or hoped to be a gem.

The third dimension is where animation has branched off into a new realm over the past 20 years, and the medium has never been the same. Whether one is creating a 2D film by hand drawing, or in the computer in Flash, or creating a 3D CG film, the visualization possibilities of working in 3D have irrevocably changed the way animation is made. Audiences are now so much more attuned to seeing animation in virtual three-dimensional space that their expectations have been altered significantly from a time when everything was basically flat. Even Disney's Multiplane system from the 1950s, where layers of animation elements were photographed in real depth, one behind the other, still created an essentially "proscenium" experience, where the audience was looking at a stage-like environment and action was taking place largely in a horizontal, right-to-left-to-right space. In addition to allowing shapes to have a greater sense of weight and dimensionality, 3D animation allows the camera to explore and to light these objects and their environments with a much greater degree of variation and movement.

The fourth dimension is the truly cinematic dimension, the dimension of time. No other art form has worked in the fourth dimension in the same way as cinema. From the early revolving zoetropes to today's high frame-rate digital projectors, the element of time, of beginning, middle, and end, is the hallmark of this medium. The editor is the high priest of the filmmaking process, taking the raw elements of shots and scenes and piecing them together to create rhythm, pace, and narrative coherency. Indeed, the juxtaposition of images, as the early master directors like Griffith and Eisenstein discovered, is the highest expression of this art form. This juxtaposition of image, and juxtaposition over time, creates emotions, from joy to sadness to suspense and fear. The addition of sound, both music and sound effects, further dimensionalizes the timeline, making the pace seem longer or slower, punctuating the visuals and improving the flow.

The fifth dimension, content, what the film is about and how it unfolds, is the keystone that brings the other dimensions together and gives them life. Without a compelling visual or dramatic narrative, the graphical elements are static, the 3D elements are distracting, and the timeline is boring or frenetic.

Every film really needs some form of beginning, middle, and end, whether it is a short tone poem or a character-driven narrative.

Key images, "movie moments," establish the tone or the essence of the film: a great opening shot, signature lighting, a musical theme. This tells us what the film is going to be about, about the world we are about to be immersed in. Remember that you are communicating with your audience. For you to touch them, you're going to have to make your expression understandable, whether this is through your use of visual language, choice of artistic style, cultural reference, or otherwise. So from the first frames, we the audience need to know where we are and feel like something is happening that is engaging. From there, the filmmaker has to stay "on point." Everything that follows must serve the purpose of the film. This process of choosing and editing what goes into the film is the most painstaking part of the process and will challenge you to really discover what it is you are actually saying in your film.

Having laid down these ground rules, it is now important to say break them! Trust your instincts, trust your experience. Don't get bogged down by anything that stands in the way of your vision. This is perhaps the most important lesson: Dare to fail, because in your failure is always the seed of your eventual success. Be open to the lessons and dare to try again.

Preface

Why Read This Book?

Story is the backbone of all film. Without a good story, all you have is technique. This book is a guide to help you make good stories for the animated short.

Why Did We Write This Book?

There are many good books that address scriptwriting, storytelling, animation, and animation technique. Most of these books focus on feature films. This book is devoted to ideas for animated shorts that are 2–5 minutes in length, produced by one individual or a small group.

When this book was proposed, there were few books like it. Our goal was to write a book that provided the basics and that was short, easy to read, and affordable.

What This Book Is and Is Not

It is not a "how-to" book that will give you a step-by-step process for a successful story. There is no magic formula for story. This book covers the things you need to think about and consider, so you will be able to recognize a good idea, make a good story, produce good designs, and make good storyboards for the animated short.

Who Should Read This Book?

This book is designed for the beginner but has information that may be useful to any animator who works with story.

What You Will Learn

- How story for animated feature films relates to story for the animated short
- How to get good ideas
- Why acting is important to the animator
- How emotion drives the actions and reactions of a character
- What makes a good character and a good character design
- What makes a good location or environment

- What to think about when building a story
- Why conflict is essential to story, character, and audience
- How to translate story into visuals for a storyboard
- What constitutes good staging for a film

Interviews Add Depth

Interviews from professionals provide insight from the industry into story, development, and storyboarding. More interviews are included on the DVD. Don't miss them.

Why Did We Choose These Animations for the DVD?

Some of the animations on the DVD are older films, some are newer films. Some are more polished or animated better than others. Some are from professional studios and some are student work. All films were chosen because they are examples of good storytelling. When possible, animatics and process work are shown on the DVD to give a fuller understanding of the development of the ideas for each film. The DVD also includes a videotape from an acting workshop that illustrates the principles in the book.

Summary

The animated short is one of the enjoyable forms of entertainment. It doesn't take too long, but can be as poignant, humorous, and moving as any other form of storytelling. Doing it well creates memories.

Acknowledgments

We would like to acknowledge the following people for their help, support, and contributions to the book:

Family:

Larry and Mack Sullivan; Milton and Helen Alexander; Barbara and Nathan Schumer

Editors:

Georgia Kennedy, Paul Temme, Elsevier

Editorial Assistant:

Chris Simpson, Elsevier

Project Manager:

Kathryn Liston, Elsevier

Proposal Reviewers:

Mark T. Byrne, Craig Caldwell, David Maas, Joseph Guilland, Alan Choi

Technical Reviewers:

Craig Caldwell and Sharon Cavanaugh

Colleagues:

Jim McCampbell, Computer Animation Faculty, and Students at Ringling College of Art and Design; Richard Hopkins and Florida Studio Theater

Contributing Students:

Meng Vue, Eric Drobile, Gwynne Olson-Wheeler, Nick Pitera, Chris Nabholtz, Thelvin Cabezas, Fernanda Santiago, Kevin Andrus, and Maria Clapis from Ringling College of Art and Design; Parrish Ley from Sheridan College; Mark Shirra and Alejandra Perez from Vancouver Film School; Chris Perry from University of Massachusetts at Amherst; Sven Martin, Moritz Mayerhofer, Jan Locher, Hannes Appell, Holger Wenzl, Jan Thuring from

Flimakademie, Baden-Wuerttemberg, Germany; Alex Cannon from Brigham Young University

Contributing Studios:

Jeff Fowler, Sean McNally, and Chuck Wojtkiewics, Blur Studios; Sande Scoredos, Sony Pictures Imagesworks; Sylvain Chomet, Django Films

Foreword:

John Tarnoff, DreamWorks Animation

Interviews:

Jeff Fowler, Blur Studios; Andrew Jiminez, Pixar Animation Studios; Kendal Cronkhite, DreamWorks Feature Animation; Kathy Alteri, DreamWorks Feature Animation; Tom Bancroft, Funnypages Productions, LLC; Chris Renaud, Blue Sky Studios; Mike Thurmeier, Blue Sky Studios; Sande Scoredos, Sony Pictures Imageworks; Nathan Greno, Walt Disney Feature Animation; Barry Cook, Story Artist and Director; Steve Gordon, Professional Story Artist; Jim Story, Instructor of Story at University of Central Florida; Paul Briggs, Walt Disney Feature Animation; Frank Gladstone, Independent Animation Consultant

Videotaping:

Phil Chiocchio

Scriptwriters:

Nick Pierce and Christianne Greiert

Actors:

Katherine Michelle Tanner, Adam Ratner, Christianne Greiert

Illustrators and Photographers:

Mike Peters, Adam D. Martens, Gary Schumer

Other Great People Who Helped Us Connect with Other People:

Patricia Galvis-Assmus, University of Massachusetts at Amherst; Brent Adams, Brigham Young University; Larry Bafia, Vancouver Film School; Thomas Haegele and Tina Ohnmacht, Flimakademie, Baden-Wuerttemberg, Germany; Marilyn Friedman, Olivier Mouroux, Fumi Kitahara, DreamWorks Feature Animation; Steven Argula, Pixar Animation Studios; Christina Witoshkin, Blue Sky Studios; Samantha Brown, Sony Pictures Imageworks; Billy Merritt, Ringling College of Art and Design; Tyson Sturgeon, Elsevier; and all of our friends who provided constant encouragement.

The Purpose of Storytelling: Analyzing *Dag and The Dinosaur*

Once, there was a great tribe that lived in caves near what is now ZhouKouDain in China.

They were not so different from what we are today. They played games, enjoyed each other's company, raised their families, and worked.

One of the toughest jobs in the tribe was hunting. The best hunter in the tribe was an Upperman named Dag. He was proud of his ability to bring in game quickly. In those days, the hunt lasted until there was a kill. The hunter would never return to the tribe without food. It would disappoint the tribe and the hunter would be disgraced. Dag was rarely out more than one day on a hunt. Because he was so good, he was appointed the task of training the new hunters in the tribe. So one day, Dag set out taking with him a new partner, Og.

Dag taught Og all that he knew, but they had not caught a single thing. They had been hunting for *four* days. They had traveled farther from the tribe than they had ever been before.

Dag was worried. In addition to being hungry themselves, they knew their tribe must be impatient and hungry as well. They were restlessly settling down by their campfire, bemoaning their bad luck, when things went from bad to worse.

Thump! Thump! Bam! Boom!

Dag and Og jumped to their feet! It happened again, Thump! Thump! Bam! Boom! From out of the brush came a large sharp-toothed monster!

They had never seen anything like it. They thought it was a dinosaur!

But it couldn't have been a dinosaur. The dinosaurs died out long ago.

It really didn't matter. Whatever it was, they were under attack.

Dag grabbed a log of fire and braced himself. Og started to run. The dinosaur moved between them. They were divided.

The dinosaur looked at Dag—he waved his fire. It looked at Og. Og ran. In one step, the dinosaur caught him and ate him up. Then it turned back toward Dag. Dag waved his fire. He screamed and waved his fire and threw it at the beast. And do you know what happened?

. . . The beast left!

Dag ran, as fast as he could, back to the tribe.

"Where is our food?" they asked, "Where is Og?"

"No, no, no, you don't understand . . . ," exclaimed Dag and he began to tell them his story.

"Og and I were settling down for the night. The hunting trip had not been going well. We were talking about our bad luck—when a dinosaur attacked us." At this the tribe laughed.

"I know, I KNOW—it couldn't have been a dinosaur—but it was something like that with big teeth! I picked up a log of fire. I don't know why—I just did."

"Og ran. Og got eaten. But me—I waved my fire! I screamed and threw my fire at the dinosaur. . . ." The tribe laughed.

"Pay attention!" shouted Dag. "I threw fire at the dinosaur! And do you know what happened?! It LEFT! I ran back here to tell you. . . ."

The tribe thought about this. They talked about it. They decided, as a group, to stay close to home and always have fire with them. They agreed to never go near the land where the dinosaur lived.

This worked really well for them for many years. But eventually the animals near their home started dwindling in numbers. They found themselves venturing farther and farther on the hunt, creeping closer and closer to the dinosaur's home.

During one hunt, Dag, and his new partner Nog, were settling down for the night. Nog was nervous. They were very close to the border of the dinosaur's home.

Dag was already asleep and Nog had finally began to relax when—Thump! Thump! Bam! Boom!

Both men started to their feet! They grabbed their flaming logs. They stood back to back. They were ready.

From the brush emerged two large feet. Attached to these feet was a huge body with large scales lining the back and flowing all the way down to the tip of a strong tail. At the top of the body was a large head with huge nostrils. From the nostrils, there were trails of smoke. It was the largest, scariest creature that Nog had ever seen.

Dag and Nog looked at each other. They were in agreement. They shoved the points of their flaming logs together and they showed the beast their fire.

Then, the beast showed them HIS fire. Nog was burned to a crisp. Poof! Just like that, ashes floated to the ground. Nothing was left.

Dag looked at his fire. He looked at the beast. He looked at Nog's ashes.

Dag dropped his fire, turned and ran all the way back to the tribe.

"Where is our food?" they asked, "Dag, did you lose another partner? Where is Nog?"

"No, no, no, you don't understand . . . ." exclaimed Dag.

"Oh no, not again!" groaned the tribe, "What about the fire?!"

"Pay attention!" shouted Dag. He began to tell them his story.

After listening, the tribe was very afraid.

The next night, they were having a vegetable barbeque with their neighbors (no one wanted to hunt anymore) when they told them their story.

"Oh, yes!" said the neighbors, "We know that beast! We had many deaths too, before we understood it. It is a dragon! It is a god. In fact, it is the god of fire and rain. It is very powerful. But it can be pleased and appeased. Do you know what we do?"

The entire tribe leaned forward to listen and asked, "What?"

"It seems strange, but it likes fruit," explained the neighbors.

"Fruit!?" cried Dag in disbelief. "Fruit?!"

"Yes, fruit. Each year, in the spring, we bring fruit and flowers to the edge of the dragon's land. We chant. We burn incense to take our chant over the border to bring the dragon to the gifts. The dragon, in return for the fruit, blows fire into the sky. Then it rains."

"The rains allow us to grow more fruit. And other crops too, like these fine vegetables we're eating tonight. We don't hunt anymore. We grow crops."

"For the gift of rain we put the dragon's image on the walls of our cave and carve it into our weapons. We respect its land. We never go there except to bring the gifts. This seems to work."

"Wow, okay," said the tribe thoughtfully, "We'll do that too. Can you pass the carrots?"

"I'll get them," said Dag as he grabbed his neighbor's hoe and headed out of the cave.

Illustration, Nick Pitera, Ringling School of Art and Design

"Can you catch carrots in one day?" he asked.

Why do we tell stories?

Illustration by Nick Pitera, Ringling College of Art and Design

Why did Dag tell stories?

At first Dag and Og told stories **to entertain** each other around the campfire, **to share their experience**, to discuss their bad luck, **to reassure each other** of their place in the tribe. Then Dag told the tribe the story of Og and the monster. He told his story so the tribe could **see the experience through his eyes**, to learn what he had learned. He told his story **to process the problem**, to create a sounding board for how the tribe should operate in the universe, **to understand the consequences of his actions**. The tribe told the stories to each other for a long time to keep each other safe, **creating tradition and history**. And finally, the tribe told its stories to others, **to explain what they didn't know**, to compare notes, to apologize for their dinner. The neighbors told stories **to teach**, to give advice, to convey information of value. All of these stories were engaging to the people telling them and the people hearing them.

There are many reasons to tell stories, but all of them have really one purpose: to show us something about ourselves. Stories are about people.

Chapter 1

Story Background and Theory

As human beings, we live in story all of the time. Story is as natural and essential to us as breathing. We all have stories to tell, but telling our personal stories on a daily basis and constructing a story from scratch are two very different things. Usually when we tell stories on a daily basis, we are relating events to one or two other people. When constructing story, we are trying to communicate with a mass audience. When we tell stories to a friend it is because it is important to us or to them. We are connected and moved emotionally because it is personal. When we construct story, we are moving not just an individual, but an audience. The goal then becomes to make the personal universal.

Before we can begin getting ideas, developing characters, or building stories, we need to understand the background of story and how that background lays the foundation for what we want to make: a story for an animated short film.

This chapter deals with story basics: the definition of story, why all stories and characters seem the same, why conflicts and themes seem similar, originality in story, and the difference between feature films and the animated short.

What Is a Story?

Screenwriter Karl Iglesias has a very simple and clear definition of story: "A story has someone who wants something badly and is having trouble getting it." [1]

This definition determines the three primary elements necessary for a story: character, character goal, and conflict. Without these elements, story cannot exist.

1. *Character.* This is whom the story is about and through whose eyes the story is told.
2. *Goal.* This is the physical object the character wants to obtain: the princess, the treasure, the girl, the boon, the bounty, the recognition, and so on.
3. *Conflict.* Conflict is what is between the character and his goal. There are three forms of conflict:
   - Character vs. Character
   - Character vs. Environment
   - Character vs. Self

Conflicts create problems, obstacles, and dilemmas that place the character in some form of danger or jeopardy, either physically, mentally or spiritually. This means that there will be something at stake for the character if they do not overcome the conflict.

The other elements of story include:

- *Location.* Stories take place in a space. Location is the place, time period, or atmosphere that supports the story.

- *Inciting Moment.* In every story, the world of the character is normal until something unexpected happens. This unexpected event begins the story.

- *Story Question.* The inciting moment will set up questions in the mind of the audience that must be answered by the end of the story.

- *Theme.* Stories have meaning to the character and to the audience. The theme or concept is the underlying larger idea that the animation communicates. It is the deeper meaning of the story. Common themes include man prevails against nature, technology advances against man, and love conquers all.

- *Need.* In order for the story to have meaning to the character, he or she needs to learn something to achieve the goal.

- *Arc.* When a character learns—or doesn't learn—there will be what is called an *emotional arc* or change in the character.

- *Ending/Resolution.* The ending is what must be given to the viewer to bring emotional relief and answer all of the questions of the story. The ending must transform the audience or the character.

As you move through the book, you will gain an understanding of how the elements of story are defined, how they function, and how they work together.

Why Do All Stories Seem the Same?

With so many different story elements and seemingly infinite ways to combine them, why do all stories seem familiar, as if you have heard them somewhere before? Why do all films seem like you've seen them before?

It is because in some form or another, you have. Nearly every story told, every feature film produced, follows the same structure and formula with similar characters, themes, and conflicts.

The lights dim. In the first 20 minutes of a movie, a hero will be introduced. He will have some flaw that makes him human—just like us. Something unexpected will happen that throws his world into chaos. For the next hour or so, our hero will go through a series of trials, aided by friends and challenged by foes, trying to restore order to his world. In the last 20 minutes our hero will be crushed, only to rally for one final showdown against his challenger. He succeeds or fails—usually succeeds. We all celebrate.

This is the basic story. Where did it come from?

The Universal Story

From the turn of the 19th century and on, there are documented discussions between writers and theorists who noticed that the similarities in story went beyond specific regions, cultures, and time periods. [2] Some of them theorized that this was because humankind had similar natural phenomena that needed to be explained. This might be the reason for similarities in theme, but didn't explain the similarities in story and plot.

All of these stories followed a three-act structure that had first been defined by Aristotle nearly 2,300 years ago. Aristotle called this structure *Plot*. Plot was not just the sequence of events in a story, but also the emotions that were necessary to move the audience through the story. In the first act, pity and empathy must be established for the hero so that the audience cares about the character and will engage in his pursuit. Then, the second act is the scene of suffering and challenge, creating fear and tension surrounding the hero and his challenges. In the final act, fear and tension are released by catharsis, the emotional release that allows for closure to end the story. [3]

In the 20th century, Joseph Campbell, an American mythology professor, writer, and orator, began to think that he understood reasons for the similarities in story that went beyond the experience of external phenomena. Campbell worked in the fields of comparative mythology and comparative religion studying stories. What he found was that there were universal images and characters that existed in *one* story shared by all cultures through all time periods. Because this story occurred again and again, he called it the monomyth—the one story, the universal story.

The monomyth told the story of a hero and is appropriately called "The Hero's Journey." Campbell's theory has many stages, but they can be summarized as follows [4]:

- *Introduce the Hero.* The hero is the character through whom the story is told. The hero is having an ordinary day in his ordinary world.
- *The Hero Has a Flaw.* The audience needs to empathize with the hero and engage in his pursuit of success. So the hero is not perfect. He suffers from pride or passion, or an error or impediment that will eventually lead to his downfall or success.
- *Unexpected Event.* Something happens to change the hero's ordinary world.
- *Call to Adventure.* The hero needs to accomplish a goal (save a princess, retrieve a treasure, collect a boon, and so forth). Often the hero is reluctant to answer the call. It is here that he meets with mentors, friends, and allies that encourage him.
- *The Quest.* The hero leaves his world in pursuit of the goal. He faces tests, trials, temptations, enemies, and challenges until he achieves his goal.
- *The Return.* The hero returns expecting rewards.
- *The Crisis.* Something is wrong. The hero is at his lowest moment.

- *The Showdown.* The hero must face one last challenge, usually of life and death against his greatest foe. He must use all that he has learned on his quest to succeed.
- *The Resolution.* In movies this is usually a happy ending. The hero succeeds and we all celebrate.

Table 1.1 Feature Film Plots Against the Hero's Journey

	Shrek	*Mulan*	*The Incredibles*	*Howl's Moving Castle*
Introduce the Hero	Shrek is an ogre who lives in a swamp and just wants to be left alone.	Mulan is the only child of the honored Chinese family, Fa.	Former Superhero, Mr. Incredible—now Bob Parr—is stuck in a dead-end job where he tries to help people, be a good dad, and fit into "normal" society.	Sophie is a girl who lives in a magical land. At a parade she is accosted by soldiers and saved by a wizard. Her friend warns, "Wizards steal the hearts of beautiful girls."
Hero Has a Weakness	Shrek is an ogre.	She's a girl. She is smart, headstrong, and loud. This is not a good combination for an honorable Chinese female.	Bob wants to fight crime—and lies about it to do so. Bigger problem: He likes to work alone.	Sophie doesn't see herself as beautiful. There are esteem issues.
Unexpected Event	Shrek's swamp is invaded by fairy tale characters displaced by Lord Farquaad. Shrek wants his swamp back. Donkey knows where Farquaad lives. Shrek is forced to go with Donkey.	Mulan's weakened father, Fa-Zous, is called to join the army and fight the Huns.	Mr. Incredible gets a secret message from a beautiful woman calling for his services to defeat a government robot gone haywire.	Sophie makes hats. The Witch of Waste visits Sophie's hat shop after hours. When Sophie won't help her, she turns Sophie into an old hag.
Call to Adventure	Farquaad gives Shrek a choice: Rescue the princess or die. Well, OK. Shrek goes to rescue the princess, but only after Farquaad promises to give him his swamp back if he does.	Knowing her father would never survive, Mulan disguises herself as a man and joins the army.	Bob takes the bait. Come on, Bob—her name is MIRAGE—see through it. He answers the call, defeats the robot, and accepts a new job—all while deceiving his family.	Unable to tell anyone she is cursed, Sophie leaves to find a way to remove it. She meets a scarecrow who gets her a job in Howl's moving castle. There she cuts a deal with a cursed fire: I'll free you if you free me.

Table 1.1 *Continued*

	Shrek	*Mulan*	*The Incredibles*	*Howl's Moving Castle*
The Quest	Shrek makes friends with Donkey, crosses rickety bridges above lava, fights a fire-breathing dragon, and rescues the princess.	With the help of a dragon and a lucky cricket, Mulan learns skills to fight the Huns under the leadership of Shang, her captain.	Fighting robots is a trap set by his rejected sidekick wanna-be Syndrome. Mr. Incredible's family finds out and sets out to rescue him.	Sophie learns Howl is a mess because he has no heart, using his powers for selfish reasons that will destroy him. He keeps turning into a bird and flying away. And there is a war going on that depends on Howl.
The Return	Shrek has to persuade the princess to go to Duloc. On the way, they fight Robin Hood and his Merry Men, play with spider web balloons, and find a place to sleep because the difficult princess insists and fall in love.	The Huns attack. Mulan starts an avalanche, defeats the Huns, saves Shang, but gets wounded in the process. Shang discovers Mulan is a girl.	Syndrome sends a robot that only he can control to the city, defeats it, and becomes the greatest superhero ever. He must be stopped.	Howl's hair is a different color. He can't go on if he's not beautiful. Sophie screams she's never been beautiful. Everyone's ugly and they get weaker and uglier.
The Crisis	Fiona, the princess, is about to marry Farquaad. Shrek has his swamp back, but is miserable. Donkey tells him to go tell Fiona he loves her before it is too late.	She is outcast. On the way home she discovers the Huns are going to attack the Emperor's city. She hurries there but no one will believe her.	But Mr. Incredible is captured. Believes his family is dead. City is in jeopardy.	Howl flies away from the castle (again). It falls apart. Howl is dying. Sophie is desperate.
The Showdown	Shrek rides the dragon to Duloc, stops the wedding, confronts Farquaad, and tells Fiona he loves her.	Huns kidnap the Emperor. Mulan defeats the Huns. Emperor offers her honor and a job. She just wants to go home. Shang still won't have anything to do with her.	Family isn't dead. They save him. Follow Syndrome to the city. Mr. Incredible wants to take on Syndrome alone. Learns he needs his family. He can't work alone.	The Witch of Waste has Howl's heart. Sophie asks her for it. OK. She gives it up. Sophie puts Howl's heart back.
Happy Ending	Fiona loves Shrek too. She turns into an ogre, Shrek gets his swamp back, and Farquaad is eaten by the dragon. The dragon and Donkey fall in love. We all celebrate.	Emperor gives Shang a good talking to. He goes after Mulan. Fa Zhou is proud. She has honor and gets the guy. We celebrate.	They save the city but Syndrome has Jack-Jack, their son. Don't worry. Jack-Jack can hold his own. Syndrome is defeated and the family is a happy unit.	Howl is fine. He loves Sophie. Sophie thinks she's beautiful. The fire is free, but chooses to stay. The scarecrow is a prince who can end the war. True love transforms everything.

Disney movies have long been constructed for a collective audience, sitting in a darkened theater that shares the experience of the hero. Disney films have driven home the opportunity of the individual to succeed and that, above all, it is personal success that we celebrate. In Disney films there is a clear hero who fights a clear villain. Nearly all of the classic Disney movies are excellent case studies of the Hero's Journey.

On the other hand, Pixar films follow every aspect of the structure except that of the Hero. If we define a hero simply as the eyes through which the story is told, then Pixar, too, more or less fits the formula. If we define the hero as the one who succeeds and whose success we celebrate, then this changes the dynamics when we look at a Pixar film.

In Pixar films, from *A Bug's Life* on, the role of hero is more often played as if it were a baton in a relay race, passing from character to character. [5] For example, in *Finding Nemo*, it is Marlin's quest to find Nemo. But Marlin fails. He begins to return home without his son. It is Nemo who brings himself home and it is Dory's role to reunite Nemo with his dad. At different times, Gill is the hero, and then Dory is the hero—each character has a unique purpose that, in the true Andy Warhol 15-minutes-of-fame theory, allows him or her to be the hero of his or her own part of the story. This, coupled with original story, is what makes a Pixar film seem concurrently familiar, yet unique and fresh. Even in *The Incredibles* there are times when the role of hero passes from character to character, even to the shape-shifting character named appropriately, Mirage.

Miyazaki also orders the events in a classic structure. However, in most of his stories the identification of good and evil is not clear. For Miyazaki, evil, if it can be called that, is that which dwells within us. His stories have conflict that is often more internalized. Success comes through personal resurrection. Through the character's personal transformation, the peace in society is restored.

Character Archetypes

In movies there are definite character roles that appear over and over in the all of the stories.

These roles come from character archetypes. An archetype is defined as a pervasive idea or image that serves as an original model from which copies are made. For our purposes, this means that there is a baseline character model that any surface or costuming can be placed upon. The hero is a baseline that can be a superhero, Mr. Incredible; an ogre, Shrek; a girl, Mulan; a woolly mammoth, Manfred, and so on.

The term first comes from Carl Jung, a 20th century psychoanalyst who studied dreams and the unconscious. Jung found that there were reoccurring images and themes running through the dreams of his patients that were so similar that they could not come from individual conflicts. He believed that these images originated in the collective unconsciousness of all people, and he called these images *archetypes*.

Jung's archetypes divided the individual into four parts or psyches: the self, the shadow, the male, and the female. These were not defined as individual characters, but as attributes common in every individual. In Jung's world, these base archetypes would manifest themselves in other forms: the female part of the psyche might be the great mother; the male part of the psyche might be the eternal child; the self might be a hero, wise old man, a trickster, and so forth. They were the different ways in which individuals would see themselves. And these formed the basis for the stories that his patients would tell.

In the stories of feature films we find the same thing. There are archetypes that form the basis of nearly all the characters in the movies we watch. *The Writer's Journey* by Chris Vogler, identifies seven archetypal characters found in most feature films:

1) The Hero—the character through which the story is told.

2) The Mentor—the ally that helps the hero.

3) The Herald—this character announces the "Call to Adventure" and delivers other important information throughout the story. This role sometimes shifts from character to character.

4) The Shadow—this is the villain or major protagonist. Sometimes, as in Miyazaki's films, the shadow resides in the character himself.

5) The Threshold Guardian—this is a character, passageway, or guardian that the hero must get past in order to proceed on the quest, or to retrieve the object of the quest. In *Shrek*, the Threshold Guardian is the dragon that guards Fiona.

6) The Trickster—this character is usually the comic relief in the story. He sometimes leads the hero off track or away from the goal.

7) The Shapeshifter—this character is not who she appears or who she presents herself to be. [6]

Archetype Silhouettes by Gary Schumer, Ringling College of Art and Design

Table 1.2 Character Archetypes in Feature Films

	Shrek	Mulan	The Incredibles	Howl's Moving Castle
The Hero	Shrek	Mulan	Bob Parr, Mr. Incredible	Sophie
The Mentor/Friend	Donkey	Mushu	Elastigirl	The Boy, Markl, Calcifer
The Herald	Farquaad's soldier, the mirror on the wall, Gingerbread man	The Ancestors	Mirage	The Scarecrow
The Shadow	Farquaad	The Huns	Syndrome	Howl
The Threshold Guardian	Dragon	Shang	The Robot	The Witch of Waste
The Trickster	Donkey	Army buddies	The Kids: Dash, Violet, Jack-Jack	Calcifer, Madam Sulimen
The Shapeshifter	Fiona	Mulan	This is a story about superheroes—everyone changes form!	Sophie, Howl, the Scarecrow

In Table 1.2 we can see how these characters manifest themselves in selected movies. Sometimes more than one role is fulfilled by the same character.

It is important to note here that an archetype is not a stereotype. Here is the difference. A stereotype is a simplified generalization about a specific group of people. Example: All elderly people have blue hair, dementia, and arthritis.

An archetype, on the other hand, is a character attribute that can manifest itself in any human (or in animation, nonhuman) body and that is a recognizable icon by the audience. For example, in *Iron Giant*, the giant is the child that has to be taught. In *Ice Age*, Manfred becomes the great mother—of both the Indian child and the "herd."

Exercise:

1. What is your favorite feature film? Watch it carefully while you track plot points against the Hero's Journey. Observe the characters and figure out which archetypal role they fulfill.

Universal Conflicts

Conflict is the situation or problem that is getting in the way of the character's goal. It is a dilemma that creates tension for the character. It is something that puts the character in jeopardy.

With all the infinite problems and predicaments that face humankind, you would think that the expressions of conflict in story would be equally infinite. But again, we find recurring motifs of conflict expressed in story. In fact, these motifs occur with such frequency that instead of recognizing these as forms of conflict, we categorize them into types of familiar stories [7]:

- *Brains vs. Brawn.* These conflicts pit intelligence against brute strength.
- *Rags to Riches.* These are stories about personal struggle for achievement.
- *Good vs. Evil.* Sets equal forces against each other.
- *Role Reversals.* Allows us to see through the eyes of the "other" and experience how others live.
- *Courage and Survival.* The conflict that is usually environmental. There is a disaster or disease that must be overcome.
- *Peacemakers.* These are underdog stories where the "good" are those who protect the weak or stand up for what is right.
- *Tempting Fate.* The conflict arises when the hero goes against the established order of things (the law, God, nature), sometimes for the greater good, but more often for personal gain.
- *Fish out of Water.* A character or characters are transported to a different time or place where they must learn how to survive.
- *Ship of Fools.* Several fully defined but distinctly different characters must navigate an adventure together.
- *Buddy Stories.* These stories focus on the strengths and contrasts of the characters to overcome adversity and become friends.
- *Love Stories.* The study of romantic relationships that focuses on the trials that bring two people together or tear them apart.
- *Quests and Journeys.* In these stories, heroes traverse space and/or time to retrieve an object or person only to find themselves changed through the experience. [7]

Often, in feature films, there will be one conflict motif that is the main conflict or problem. Then there may be secondary motifs that emerge in the subplots. Below are some examples:

Examples:

MOVIE	PRIMARY CONFLICT	SECONDARY CONFLICT	TERTIARY CONFLICT
Iron Giant	Fish out of Water	Buddy Story	Peacemakers
Mulan	Fish out of Water	Courage and Survival	Love Story
Ice Age	Ship of Fools That Become Buddies	Peacemakers	Brains vs. Brawn
The Triplets of Belleville	Love Story	Fish out of Water	Good vs. Evil
Shrek	Role Reversals	Love Story	Quest
The Incredibles	Good vs. Evil	Tempting Fate	Ship of Fools
Howl's Moving Castle	Courage and Survival	Good vs. Evil	Ship of Fools

Universal Themes

Stories have meanings. They are not just a series of events. They communicate something to us that is larger than the story itself. The meaning or dominant idea of the story is called the *theme*.

Themes are often based on human needs. These needs fall into three categories:

1. Physical needs
2. Mental needs
3. Spiritual needs

Within these three categories we find the basic needs of:

- Food
- Shelter
- Security
- Acceptance
- Stimulus
- Love
- Order

This limited number of needs forms nearly all of the themes of our stories. In feature films, there is usually one main theme that drives the movie. There are multiple subthemes that drive scenes and secondary character relationships.

To understand this better, we are going to look at seven major animated feature films from different studios and parts of the world: *Iron Giant* (Warner), *Mulan* (Disney), *Shrek* (Dream-Works), *Ice Age* (Blue Sky), *The Triplets of Belleville* (Chomet), *The Incredibles* (Pixar), and *Howl's Moving Castle* (Miyazaki).

Sometimes, movies are generous enough to actually tell you the main theme if you are listening. In *Iron Giant*, the main theme of the movie is "You are what you choose to be." This is what Dean, the scrap-metal artist, tells Hogarth Hughes as he rants about his classmates. Hogarth then teaches it to the Giant who repeats it to himself. At the climax of the film, the Giant has transformed into a very large, defensive weapon when Hogarth reminds him that he doesn't have to be a weapon, "You are what you choose to be." The giant chooses to be a hero—like Superman. This theme is based on the need for meaning, security, and acceptance.

At the end of the movie *Mulan*, the Chinese Emperor admonishes Mulan: "I have heard a great deal about you, Fa Mulan. You stole your father's armor, ran away from home, impersonated a soldier, deceived your commanding officer, dishonored the Chinese army, *destroyed my palace!* . . . and you have saved us all." As Mulan heads for home, the

Emperor tells Shang (Mulan's commanding officer and love interest), "A flower that blooms in adversity is the rarest and most beautiful of all." This communicates the needs of acceptance, love, and order.

For other movies, it is not so obvious. You really have to think about what the movie is saying. Sometimes, if you look at what the main character wants and what he or she needs to learn, it often points you to the theme. It is not the objective of a movie to have the audience leave the theater spouting themes—"Wow! That *Shrek!* A person's worth is measured by character! Remind me to realign my ethics!" It is the job of the film to move them unconsciously toward the theme through their emotions. "I love that story. I want to watch it over and over again. If an ogre deserves love, maybe I do, too." However, as a creator of films, it is really useful to know what you are trying to say in your film.

Let's look at some other films whose themes you need to think about:

The Triplets of Belleville: On the surface, this almost seems cliché: Love will defeat all odds (even the French mafia). But this is actually too simplistic. *Triplets* is a complicated film that also comments on parenting, the world of sports, the world of arts and class systems, and more.

Ice Age: A herd sticks together. Families are made up of all types of creatures, whose combined strengths and weaknesses make us whole.

The Incredibles: A herd sticks together. No really . . . Mr. Incredible can't work alone . . . strengths, weaknesses make us whole. Mr. Incredible must learn that he needs help to be a successful superhero.

Howl's Moving Castle: A herd sticks together . . . a person's worth lies in his or her character . . . love will defeat all odds. Think about it.

Exercise: Go to your local video store. Video stores usually have shelves that house the employees' favorite movies. Or they will have a second shelf of older movies near a bestseller. If the bestseller is sold out, but you wanted that movie, you will probably like this other movie, too. See how many of them have similar main themes.

Originality in Story

If there are limited themes, conflicts, structures, and character types, what makes each story unique?

Robert McKee states that story is about form, not formula. It is completely possible to have good story structure and still not have a good story. While the themes, conflict, structures, and archetypes may be the same, what is unique is a compelling character and emotionally driven sequence of events. Each character will react to events in a different way. Observing how someone else reacts to problems, different from how we, as an audience member might, is concurrently educational and compelling. It gives us a reason to watch.

The other thing that makes a unique story is character *desire*. In the section on theme, we discussed basic character needs. Often what we want or desire is not what we need. Therefore, conflict in story can be about desire vs. need. Desire is often unrealistic. It is complicated by greed, pride, ambition, fear, laziness, apathy, and so forth. To be successful, characters must overcome desire and learn what they need.

Example: Shrek wants (desire) to be left alone, but what he needs to learn is that he needs others, and he deserves others. Manfred just wants to be left alone, but he finds he needs a herd. Howl wants to be left alone, but finds he needs his heart (and thus others).

What makes a story interesting for an audience is the ability to engage with a character and either vicariously, voyeuristically, or viscerally, watch the unique ways that that character reacts to the problems and obstacles he or she confronts.

Making the Long Story Short: The Difference between Features and Shorts

Beyond the obvious differences in running time, scope, complexity, budget and resources, the animated short requires a directness, clarity, simplicity, and economy of structure, plot, and assets not found in feature films.

Initial ideas for a short are often too big, too complicated, and cover too much territory. It's not hard to see why. Most of our references are based on the hero's journey.

In the hero's journey, the characters (many of them) meet with conflict (several events in several locations), until they reach a crisis (of monumental spiritual or physical proportions) where they learn a lesson (the many themes and subtexts converge), make a decision (which calls for more action), and succeed (usually in celebration with the many other characters).

So how many characters, conflicts, themes, locations, and props should a short have?

For the individual filmmaker, the short should have one theme or concept that the piece communicates and one conflict that intensifies or gets worse. It should have one or two characters, one or two locations, and only props necessary to populate the scene appropriately or drive the story forward.

The inciting moment, the moment when something unexpected happens for the character, usually occurs within the first 10–15 seconds of the film. An example is found in Eric Drobile's *The Animator and the Seat* when the chair begins to massage the animator's shoulders. Sometimes the inciting moment happens before the film even starts. In *A Great Big Robot from Outer Space Ate My Homework*, we enter the film after the alien has eaten the homework and when the boy is rushing to relate this event to his teacher.

The Animator and the Seat **by Eric Drobile, Ringling College of Art and Design;** *A Great Big Robot from Outer Space Ate My Homework,* **by Mark Shirra, Vancouver Film School**

In the short, the character will *arc*, which means she will change emotionally from the beginning to the end of the piece. But he doesn't always learn, make big decisions or even succeed. Sometimes it is enough to retrieve an object, understand an environment, solve a problem, reveal a secret, or discover something new. Shorts can be as small as a one-liner or a single gag as in *Caps* or the *Kuhfo* series.

Remember our most basic definition of a story: a character wants something badly and is having trouble getting it. When you are looking for ideas, this is the basis of what you are looking for.

Let's work this definition a little bit further:

The short story has ONE character that wants something badly and is having trouble getting it. That "trouble" is, at most, ONE other character or environment that causes conflict. The resolution to the conflict communicates ONE specific idea, theme, or concept.

Kuhfo, directed by Hannes Appell and Holger Wenzl; Caps, directed by Moritz Mayerhofer and Jan Locher, Filmakademie Baden-Wuerttemberg, Germany

This will translate into the following structure:

- A *character wants* something badly
- Something happens that moves him to *action*
- He meets with *conflict*
- Things gets worse until the character is in *crisis*
- He nearly *loses* all
- Learns a *lesson*
- Makes a *hard choice*
- In order to *succeed*

When reading the following chapters, keep this simplicity in mind.

Summary

Why do we tell stories?

- To entertain
- To teach
- To compare our existence to others'
- To communicate with others
- To see the world through the eyes of others
- To learn how to be human

Many stories seem to be the same as other stories because:

- There is an archetypal story structure
- There are a limited number of archetypal characters
- There are limited number of conflicts
- There are a limited number of themes

Original stories are created through the audience's engagement in unique characters and the way that they react to and solve the conflicts they encounter.

As filmmakers, we deliver emotion. It is through emotional engagement that we move an audience.

When making the animated short, the story needs to have limited characters, limited locations, one conflict, and one theme.

Recommended Readings

Joseph Campbell, *Hero with a Thousand Faces*

The Writer's Journey by Chris Vogler

Notes

[1]Karl Iglesias, *Writing for Emotional Impact*, WingSpan Press, Livermore, CA.

[2]Christopher Booker, *The Seven Basic Plots*, Continuum, New York, NY, 2004, pp. 8–10.

[3]http://classics.mit.edu/Aristotle/poetics.1.1.html. In addition to 1) Plot, Aristotle defined four other elements of story. These are 2) Thought, which is dialogue; 3) Diction, which is the way the dialogue is said; 4) Sound, which is the soundtrack; and 5) Spectacle, which is the equivalent to special effects. Of these elements Spectacle was the least important. It seems that even Aristotle realized that effects are only good if the audience is not distracted by them.

[4]This is a modified version of the Hero's Journey as defined by Chris Vogler in his book, *The Writer's Journey*. In his book is an excellent chart that compares Vogler's Map of the Hero's Journey as compared to Campbell's. See Christopher Vogler, *The Writer's Journey*, Michael Wiese Productions, Studio City, CA, p. 16.

[5]Ed Hooks, Newsletter, Acting Notes, CA.

[6]*The Writer's Journey*, Chris Vogler, Michael Wiese Productions, Studio City, CA.

[7]John Douglas, Glenn P. Harnden, *The Art of Technique: An Aesthetic Approach to Film and Video Production*, Allyn and Bacon, A Simon & Schuster Company, Needham, MA, 1996, pp. 16–20.

The Ideas behind *Gopher Broke*: An Interview with Jeff Fowler, Blur Studios

Jeff Fowler is a writer, director, layout supervisor, and animator at Blur Studios. Jeff wrote and directed Blur's short film, *Gopher Broke*, which was nominated for an Academy Award for Best Animated Short Film. While at Blur Studios, Jeff has served as a Lead Character Animator and Layout Artist for Walt Disney's *Mickey's Twice Upon a Christmas*, Blur Studios *Rockfish*, and directed animation for the theatrical teaser trailer for Twentieth Century Fox's *Simpsons Movie*. He is currently working on the Warner Bros.' film adaption of Maurice Sendak's children's book classic, *Where the Wild Things Are*. Jeff graduated with honors from the Ringling School of Art and Design in Sarasota, Florida, and has won several awards for his own independent animated short films.

Small rodents performing broad physical comedy. *Gopher Broke*, directed by Jeff Fowler, Blur Studios.

Q: What is the role of the short in industry?

Jeff: Shorts are tremendously useful in animation studios to promote internal growth, both creatively and technically. A short film project offers a vehicle for research and development on a variety of tools and techniques necessary to fine-tune a studio's production pipeline. More importantly, however, they offer artists a chance to stretch their creative wings. Rarely do production artists have as much input on contract work as they do on a short film, providing a much-relished opportunity to influence artistic direction. Every short film we've created at Blur Studios has benefited tremendously from the enthusiasm of its artists devoting long hours in tight schedules to prove their creative mettle. The shorts programs I've been involved with have always become a labor of love, an instrument of artistic determination. The greatest, most humbling experience of my professional life has been to witness a crew of friends and colleagues devote themselves fully to seeing an idea of mine through to completion. For helping to bear the burden of that process, and for their trust and tireless efforts, I'll always be indebted to my team on *Gopher Broke*.

Outside of the shorts programs backed by animation studios, I think short films themselves offer a wonderful opportunity for creative expression to those brave enough to take them on. I've known many artists who've began short film projects in their personal time as a form of creative release. That being said, I don't know many artists who've actually *finished* their projects, but they seemed to have enjoyed the experience nevertheless! And why not? Personal short films offer an amazing opportunity to drive your own ship and enjoy complete creative control over a project, notions rarely available in the industry nowadays. It's hard to go off-schedule or over-budget when there are no schedules or budgets! (Although I'd recommend even personal short filmmakers make some attempt at producing their own efforts!)

Q: What were your goals when creating *Gopher Broke*?

My goals were to create something simple, something funny, and something I could show to my mother. The simpler the idea was, the more likely I'd be able to keep it under control as a first-time director. In the economic/budgeting sense of the word, simple means as few characters with as few locations/environments necessary to tell the story. In order for the project to be feasible for the number of artists available, its running time needed to be kept in the neighborhood of 5 minutes or less. As much as we'd all like to live in a world devoid of creative restrictions, it can be good real-world experience to endure external constraints from time to time. In retrospect, I don't think "Gopher Broke" would have *needed* to be longer than 5 minutes, but left to my own devices, who knows what overly extravagant choices I'd have made? (Rodent chariot races? Three-way gopher/farmer/alien climatic battle?) Some day I'll release a *Gopher Broke: Redux* edition which will include the scene featuring a gopher arriving in a fantastic time portal from the future in an effort to warn the present-day gopher about his impending failures. Look for it in 2010!!

Of course, as simple as a story like *Gopher Broke* seemed on the surface, there is *always* more complexity to a project than you originally think. (A gopher needs fur, a chicken needs feathers, and a horde of crows needs a LOT of feathers.) Beyond the technical, the process of story wrangling often continues through pre-production and sometimes rears its ugly head in the early phases of production as well. The moral being, your idea will almost always *grow* beyond its original scope, both technically and creatively. (For better or worse!) By starting simple, you allow yourself and your idea room to expand naturally, which is a MUCH more enviable place than committing to a large and convoluted idea which you may ultimately be forced to slice and dice for one reason or another. *(Money, time, resources.)* Better to start simple and build!

As far as the remaining goals of "something funny" and "something I could show to my mother." You don't know my mother well enough, so you'll just have to take my word that she enjoys small rodents performing broad physical comedy. That leaves the goal of "something funny," which is actually an easy item to explain. Comedy is so subjective that you really can't do much beyond trying to amuse yourself. Here's the tricky part, though; the gags and comedy will be the *first* thing to dry up in your well of enthusiasm. How funny is a joke the 300th time you've heard it? My point being, as a filmmaker you'll numb over quickly—show it to friends to reinvigorate your confidence in the material! Since we're on this whole business of goals, it's definitely a great idea to set a few for yourself if you choose to undertake a personal short film. Combine short-term with long-term (I want my main character designed by _____, I want the story reel finished and ready to be presented by _____). Even if you miss your deadlines, you'll most likely have made better progress because of them!

Chapter 2
Building Better Content

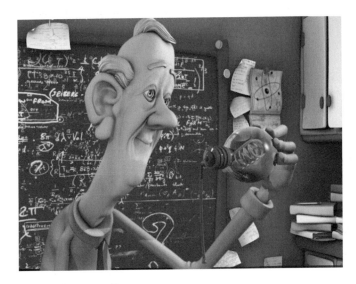

Eureka!, **by Parrish Ley, Sheridan College**

For every project, whether it is a short exercise or a feature film, you will need to get a good idea. But where do good ideas come from? How do you know when an idea is good? And if it is a good idea, is it good for the animated short?

In this chapter, you will find some guidelines. They should help you find memorable ideas that are worth the time and effort it will take to animate them.

The examples are taken from the DVD and they will make more sense to you if you've seen the animations.

Before You Begin

You are not looking for just any type of original idea, or even any type of story idea. You are looking for an idea for the animated short. Before you begin "getting ideas," it is helpful to know the rules of the playground.

Defining the Animated Short

Animations are completed constructed films that tell stories through movement and time, through memorable characters living the exaggeration of life in a representation of the world with the ability to make the invisible visible and the impossible possible.

The *short* in film is defined as anything that is 24 minutes or less. In animation, commercial shorts that run 6–11 minutes are created by teams of employees with bigger budgets and resources. For our purposes, we are defining the short as what is feasible for the individual animator. This is a running time of 1–3 minutes following a linear narrative structure.

However, the size of the short is ultimately determined by the story you need to tell. It depends on whether you are working alone or in a group, the amount of time you have, and the amount of time you are willing to spend until you send your product into the world. It depends on your resources. In addition, it depends on how much information and complexity you can handle, both conceptually and technically, and still move an audience emotionally.

The Rules of the Playground

Rule #1: Story Is King

In animation, story will infuse all the work that you do. As a shorts producer, you may well wear all the hats of production: writer, director, concept artist, storyboard artist, modeler, rigger, animator, lighting and texturing technician, sound director, and editor. In industry, you may wear only one. What ties all of these positions together is the story.

Every production element in a film is purposefully designed for the good of the story. The model needs to support the story in both style and function. The rig must allow the model to hit the exaggeration of pose or action required by the story. It is your job to understand the content you are working on and heighten it in terms of story.

It is through story that your character is revealed and that you communicate with your audience. Without story, all you have is technique.

That is not to say that technique and skill are not important. They are crucial. However, there are times when an audience (not an employer) will forgive poor technique, but they will never forgive a poor story.

Rule #2: Keep It Simple

Remember, one concept or theme, one conflict, two characters, two locations, and only the props that are needed to tell the story.

What types of stories work for the short?

- Simple single situations
- One conflict that intensifies

- A single memorable moment
  Ed Hooks, author of *Acting for Animators*, calls a memorable moment an *adrenaline moment*, [1] something that happens to the character that is of such great emotional significance that he or she will remember it when he or she is 90, such as the day I tried to fly my kite, but it flew me; the day I found true love; the day that my differences paid off.
- Slices of life
- Demonstrations of personality

The Kite by Gwynne Olson-Wheeler, Ringling College of Art and Design; *The Dancing Thief*, by Meng Vue, Ringling College of Art and Design; *Fantasia Taurina* by Alejandra Perez, Vancouver Film School

What types of stories don't work for the short?

- Hero's Journeys
- Epic Tales
- Uncharted Territories or Complicated Concepts
  You will spend all of your time in exposition, explaining where we are or how it works.
- Little-Known Facts
  You may know that penguins rub oil from a gland to make their feathers waterproof and windproof, but if your story conflict is that a penguin has run out of oil, most people will never get it.

Rule #3: Know Your Concept, Theme, or Meaning

Remember that stories have meaning. The concept is the basic overriding theme or meaning of your piece. It is not the premise or plot of the piece. It is the broader idea underneath the piece. For any concept, there could be many different narratives that communicate it.

Let's look at some possible examples:

1. *The Animator and the Seat*
   Concept: There are no breaks during crunch time.
   Premise: A tired animator attempts to take a break when he is stopped by an unexpected authority.

2. *The Kite*
   Concept: Learn to let go.
   Premise: A small creature wants to fly a kite, only the kite flies him.

3. *Eureka!*
   Concept: Inspiration comes from unexpected places.
   Premise: What happens when your usual method of getting ideas doesn't work? A genius discovers an unconventional way to get ideas.

The concept statement is one sentence. For the short, that sentence needs to be simple and clear. It needs to have a viewpoint. There is little time in the short to present an unbiased and balanced commentary.

The concept statement is the one non-negotiable element of your story. Everything else is swappable—characters, locations, plots. However, what you want to say, your theme, is your foundation. Write it down. Print it out. Read it.

Rule #4: Avoid Cliché

A cliché is a concept, character, symbol, or plot device that has been so overused that it has lost its originality.

Here are some examples:

Concepts:

- Love conquers all
- Technology bad
- Nature good

Characters:

- Robots
- Aliens
- Mimes
- Ninjas
- Fairies
- Dragons
- Pirates
- Superheroes
- Big-breasted women with guns

Symbols:

- Butterflies
- Open windows
- Chessboards
- Sunsets
- Gravestones

Plots:

- It was all a dream.
- Country mouse (or woodland animals) in the city or vice versa.
- A child's imagination (usually with monsters or imaginary friends) takes her on an adventure.
- Little kid learns something that makes him grow up.
- A lonely or neglected kid makes a robot friend.
- A character must choose between two pathways or doorways.

In an effort to be clear, immediate and accessible, it is easy to default to cliché. If you have heard it before, stop and rethink it. If you choose to use something that is considered cliché, you have to find a way to make it fresh and original—to use it in a way that has not been done before. Research and know your references. Strive to be memorable.

Rule #5: Create a Memorable Character

Shrek, Hogarth, Nemo, Woody, Howl—we remember them all. Why?

Memorable characters are ordinary enough for the audience to relate to them. They are flawed. Their flaws make them concurrently unique and accessible.

There is "something" about their design and their personality that makes us want to know more about them and makes us empathize with their plight. This is called *appeal*.

In the short, we rarely even know the character's name. Still, they stick with us for the same reasons. Memorable characters are characters that we care about.

The test of a good character is that he cannot be replaced in the story with someone or something else. Replaceable characters are flat. You can swap them out (a boy for a girl or a squirrel for a squid) and it doesn't seem to matter to the story; but, when you find the right character, it is difficult to extract him from the story because it is *his* story.

Poor Bogo, **by Thelvin Cabezas, Ringling College of Art and Design**

Rule #6: Emotion Drives Action

A story is defined by the character. More specifically, it is defined by how the character *reacts* to the situation he is in.

In film, unlike literature, the story is told through the actions of the characters. We are seldom privy to the character's thoughts. As Ed Hooks reminds us, a character will play an action until something happens to make him or her play another action. [2]

For example: I will sit and type at my computer until the phone rings and I go to answer it, or the phone might ring and I ignore it and keep typing. What I do will depend on what I am writing and how I *feel* about it, or who is calling and how I *feel* about talking to that person. I might even really like what I'm writing and ignore the phone until the fourth ring before the answering machine picks up. At this point, I make a mad dash for the phone because, *emotionally*, I can't stand not to answer it.

Too often, beginning storytellers will create the events of their story by what the character does and the action he takes instead of looking at the emotional changes in the character as he meets the rising conflicts in the story. This leads to the perception that the story is shorter in running time than it actually is. The time it takes to convey emotion and to react to a situation will grow the length your piece.

Action never just happens. Action is the *result* of thought and emotion.

What a character thinks and feels at any moment in the story is called *internal dialogue*.

"My Tomato!," *Gopher Broke* **crow, Illustration by Sean McNally, Blur Studios**

Rule #7: Show, Don't Tell

This is a golden rule of both literature and film. "Telling" means the use of exposition or description without engaging the emotional or sensory experiences of the character. Showing means to make clearly evident, by the appearance, behavior, action, or reaction, the emotional experience of the character.

Example:

Telling: As a captive princess screams for help, a young dragon prepares to defeat the approaching knights. At first he is victorious, but then one clever knight rescues the princess.

Showing: When the princess screams for help, a young dragon's muscles tighten as he braces himself against the attack of the black knight. Blowing flames from his nose, he plucks the knight from the saddle of his steed and flings him joyously in the air. With one good whack of his tail, he sends the knight over the side of the cliff. His victorious roar is cut short by a second knight riding between his legs. He panics, and turns only to find the princess has been rescued! He cowers as his sleeping father awakes to the chaos.

This isn't just more description. It includes both the emotional and visceral reactions of the dragon.

Ritterschlag, directed by Sven Martin, Filmakademie Baden-Wuerttemberg, Germany

In film, show, don't tell, means that actions speak louder than signs, voice-overs, or dialogue. In the animated short, where there is often little or no dialogue, the question of what we see becomes critical. As an animator, you need to consider not only what the character does, but the extremes of the action to communicate believably the emotion through pantomime. How are you going to employ the unique characteristics of animation in your piece? When someone asks you why you are using animation to create a film—with the time and expense involved—there needs to be a good reason. There needs to be something in the design and the storyline of your piece that *requires* animation.

This could be exaggeration, caricature, or process. Sometimes animation is a better medium to use because of the content you wish to convey. Using anthropomorphic animals allows us to look at our human characteristics, our failings and shortcomings that otherwise would be difficult to watch.

You need to consider, from the initial idea, what we are going to see. It is never too soon to begin to make your piece visual. It is often the visual that sells the idea. Sometimes, a great idea seems great—until you see the visual. Then it clearly falls flat.

Don't just write. Draw. We make images.

Rule #8: Create Conflict

This may seem obvious given our base definition of story. But often an initial pitch will include wonderful characters that are moving through events, but it is all exposition. There is no conflict and, consequently, there is no ending because there is nothing to resolve.

In *Respire, Mon Ami*, there is a little boy who is lonely but this conflict is resolved in the inciting moment when he finds a severed head at the base of the guillotine. From that moment until the boy believes his friend has "died," we have nothing but exposition as we build the relationship between the boy and the head. If the head did not expire, we would never have a conflict.

Respire, Mon Ami by Chris Nab-holtz, Ringling College of Art and Design

Conflict = Drama.

Remember that there are three, and only three, kinds of conflict:

1. Character vs. Character
   Characters need opposing goals. If both characters want the same thing, there is either:
   a) no conflict, or b) you can tell the story with one character.

2. Character vs. Environment
   The character must struggle against the environment.

3. Character vs. Self
   This is the hardest to animate because the conflict is internal. *Eureka!* does a good job of
   making an internal conflict (the need to think of an idea, to solve a problem) external-
   ized in the light bulb above the professor's head. When the normal process or pathway
   to creativity is broken, the professor flails wildly in frustration, unaware that the source
   of her ideas is still there. Order is restored only when a new pathway is achieved.

When discussing conflict, it is also necessary to discuss what conflict is not. Conflict is not a sword
fight, a war, a car chase, or a competition. These are the *results* of the character in opposition.

Rule #9: Know Your Ending

You can't really tell your story until you know the ending. Sometimes the idea you find will be the ending—the punch line or the payoff. Endings must transform the character, the audience, or both.

Rule #10: Entertain Your Audience

Audiences are entertained when they are visually, intellectually, and emotionally engaged.

When audiences watch a film, they trust you to take them on a journey and bring them back safely. They will suspend disbelief and travel with you as long as you maintain the rules of your world and keep the story truthful and the characters believable.

The best shorts are the ones that have some adventure, some sorrow, some tenderness, and some laughter. They are the ones that hold a few surprises and the ones that you continue to think about after you see them. How will your audience feel and what will they remember after watching your film?

Rule #11: Use Humor

Most people, when they think of humor and animation, think of Tex Avery, Chuck Jones, sight gags, and visual puns. Humor can also be parody, satire, or pathos.

The best humor in a short is the type that grows out of the situation, reinforces the conflict or emotion of the characters, or subtly reveals more about the character. It is sometimes funny, sometimes nervous, and sometimes empathetic.

In *Respire, Mon Ami,* the young boy tries to revive his friend with mouth-to-mouth resuscitation. In this scene, humor comes from three sources: 1) from the logical knowledge that the head is already dead and cannot be revived, 2) from the grossness (for lack of a better word) of the act itself, and from 3) the breath of the boy escaping out the neck to rustle the leaves on the ground.

Respire, Mon Ami, by Chris Nabholz, Ringling College of Art and Design

A similar example is found in *Ritterschlag* when the young dragon fails to hit the rescuing knight hard enough to force him off the cliff. When the adult dragon picks the knight up and shows it to the young dragon, the knight's leg falls off.

The falling leg helps punctuate the young dragon's shortcomings and illustrate why it is necessary to get the knight off the cliff.

Ritterschlag, directed by Sven Martin, Filmakademie Baden-Wuerttemberg, Germany

Both of these examples are comic relief, and emotional release, in what would otherwise be questionable situations even in animation.

Humor can come from empathy and failure as we watch a character attempt to fly a kite. It can come from the realization that a thief, against all better judgment, chooses to dance—and win.

It can come from the burp of a Cap who has drunk the magic potion. Burps, farts, and body popular forms of humor. We can point to numerous feature films that include them. However, if you analyze these carefully, these kinds of jokes are usually secondary humor. They are not the primary content that drives the scene. If they are, they are related to the situation in which they occur and what is poignant is not the burp or fart itself, but the *reaction* to it.

Caps, directed by Moritz Mayerhofer and Jan Locher, Filmakademie Baden-Wuerttemberg, Germany, and *Early Bloomer*, directed by Sande Scoredos, Sony Pictures Imageworks.

When looking for ideas, consider how you might make your audience laugh. This doesn't mean your piece has to be funny. Laughter comes from recognition, appeal, and reaction. It is an important consideration, since laughter is an expectation of the animated film.

Rule #12: Do Something You Like

If you don't like what you are doing, it will show in the work and no one else will like it either. Choose something that you like, that can sustain you for the months it will take to produce it. Use your own life. Nothing can quite replace personal experience to infuse a scene or a short.

Finally, for every rule, there is an exception to the rule. Learn the rules and then break them.

Getting Ideas

So, now that we know the rules of the playground, where do good ideas come from?

Kevin Andrus, Ringling College of Art and Design

The Ideal

The most linear path for getting and developing ideas comes from knowing your concept first. If you know what your piece is about, it is easy to determine early on which elements you need to tell your story: the situation that will *best* convey your message, the characters that will be in conflict with your situation, and then, your genre, time period, lighting, costuming, and everything else.

This is the most straightforward approach because your theme or concept is what drives everything else in your piece. It is the sounding board against which you place your possibilities and if your possibilities do not support your concept, you eliminate them.

Chris Perry's piece *Catch* is an example of a piece that started with a concept:

***Catch* by Chris Perry, University of Massachusetts at Amherst**

"Catch really grew out of a statistic I heard a while back. I think it was something like '50% of all middle school girls are on a diet.' This came up in the context of a conversation about how advertising succeeds at making people, especially girls, feel unhappy with themselves.

At the time I heard this, I knew I was going to have a little girl and I pictured her wandering through fields of giant billboards that were coming to life, reaching down and trying to snare her in their wicked grasp. But she was trying to chase this little ball as it rolled underneath the billboards, and she was so small they couldn't grab her.

The simplicity of *Catch* is deliberate: I wanted the advertisement image to stand out as striking and unusual because such images don't stand out in our everyday existence (and they should). The models used in advertisements represent the smallest sample of what women's bodies really look like, and the money spent to craft the perfect image defies the final result's impromptu, casual appearance.

The story basically was intact from the storyboard phase on, though I did have her try throwing the ball at the tree while lying on her back (something I used to do when I was a kid). But that was too hard to stage clearly so I switched it for the throwing game. The little gag about the sagging breast was an exception: it came up between storyboarding and animation when I was acting out that key moment of the film and trying to figure out how to visually show that this new breast wasn't doing anything for her. It was also always part of the film that gaining the adult-like chest required the removal of the ball game (putting those two desires completely against each other, so she couldn't have both).

The primary statement of *Catch* to me is about being yourself. If the film works, it works because when she is standing still with a big chest and doing nothing; it is a complete and absurd contrast to her activeness and creativity at the start of the film. "Is this what being like that person in the picture is like? How dull!" (inner monologue)."

The Real

More often than not, we start with a seed or inspiration from somewhere or something else. It could be a character design we have drawn, a location we have seen or a situation we have experienced. All of these are harder, but more visual places to start. It just takes a little more work to find the essence of your piece.

When starting with a character, you will need to figure out whom that character is and then fabricate a situation that will put him in conflict. If this is where you are at in the process, you may want to jump to Chapter 4: Building Characters and Location.

When starting with a location, you need to discover why you are attracted to it and what potential it has for story. Populate it with characters. What do they do there? What would disrupt what they usually do? If the location is generally familiar, what has changed or what is out of place that creates implication or questions in your audience's mind? What is the atmosphere of the place and what does that mean? In *The Triplets of Belleville*, three great cities, New York, Montreal, and Paris, were combined to create a place that felt familiar and communicated a sense of prosperity. The entire city creates the feeling of accumulation by contrasting the poverty of Mme. Souza and her dog to the wealth, materialism, and scale of the city and its people.

Evgeni Tomov, Art Director on *Belleville*, describes it like this, "The direction Sylvain Chomet gave me, he told me it should be a very interesting city, where there is an abundance cult for consumerism and food is a typical thing. And that's why you see so many obese people, and the characters in Belleville—you can see it for yourself—represent this over-consumerism." [3]

The Triplets of Belleville, directed by Sylvain Chomet

Sometimes, the location can tell the whole story. Ray Bradbury wrote the short story, "There Will Come Soft Rains," which follows the functions of a "smart house" long after the residents have died. Through the house itself, the lives of the people who lived there are revealed and the purpose of the house to take care of them and protect them is put in jeopardy. [4] There are a lot of mechanical devices and effects to watch that could make this good for animation. One of the hardest things about telling a story through a location is determining what is going to move.

When starting with a situation, you have to create conflict. Two people at a table having a conversation is a situation. Two people at a table fighting over the check is a conflict. To make this stronger, there has to be something at stake. What does it mean to each of these characters if he or she does not pay the bill for the other? What could make this better for animation than live action? What are the extremes that the characters go to win the conflict? What other situations are similar that could tell the story better?

When you have nothing . . . Sometimes we just don't think we have a place to start.

1. Start with Yourself

There is no better source of story than you: what you like; what you don't like; and what you know. Since story is driven by emotion start with that. What makes you happy, mad, sad, glad, frustrated, surprised, or hopeful? What is the one thing you would change about the world if you could? If you could plan the perfect day, what would it be? What is your biggest wish? What is your biggest secret? What is something you've always wanted to do but haven't? What is one thing you always wanted to do, but your body type wouldn't allow you to be good at? Be your own character.

2. Ask Why?

Look at the assumptions in your life. Why are things the way they are? Turn them over. Look at them from another viewpoint. Monsters have hidden under children's beds and in children's closets for decades, maybe centuries. Everyone knows they are there to scare young children. But no one until Pixar, with *Monsters, Inc.*, asked why? What's in it for the monsters? It's their job. But what is the payoff for doing this? Ah . . . it is their source of power. Brilliant.

3. Go into the World and Watch

Observation is one of an animator's greatest tools. The world is full of people in conflict—from the simple choice of paper or plastic, to climbing Mt. Everest. And people do the craziest things for the silliest reasons. The human race is full of emotions, logic, faults, quirks, and fallacies, which all make great fodder for animation. They have great movements, expressions, walks, and weight shifts. Sometimes something as simple as an interesting walk can reveal a character and launch a story.

4. Create Some Innocent Trouble

When we are in negotiation, we are emotionally involved and rarely have the opportunity to observe the reactions and emotions of ourselves and other people. At the grocery store, when the cashier asks if you want paper or plastic, reply, "both." Then proceed to be very specific about which items you want in paper and which you want in plastic. Watch how they react. See if they will do it. Be careful not to push too far. You are doing a study, not getting into trouble. [5]

5. Read the Newspaper

The newspaper is full of stories. That's what a paper is—current stories. Search it for something small and unique. Look at the photographs. Imagine how those people arrived at that very moment in time. What came before, what comes after?

6. Look at Art

Look at lots of art. What attracts you? Why? Is it color, composition, light, subject matter? Cezanne told story through light. Brancusi created flight out of stone. Each piece of art tells a story. If you lay that story over time, what is it?

7. Make an Adaptation of Another Story

You don't want to illustrate another story, but use it as inspiration or reference. What is the essence or concept of the story? What are parallel situations and conflicts? How can you translate it into your own form? What if you tell the same story from another viewpoint? Tell Little Red Riding Hood from the viewpoint of the wolf or the basket or the path. Don't be afraid to steal the essence of another story. Remember that there are really just a limited number of stories recreated in new forms. Without Cinderella, we wouldn't have Pretty Woman.

8. Parody a Current Story or Event

A parody is a humorous imitation that makes fun of or mocks someone, or something, like an event. It is closely related to satire. Satire is more biting than parody. It plays in the world of irony, sarcasm, and sometimes ridicule. Political figures are frequently the subject of parody and satire.

9. Create a Competition, Play with Status

In conflict, we talked about characters that have opposing goals. Sometimes, in stories of competition, characters have the same goal and are pitted against each other to reach it. These stories often use status relationships (who has power) and status often transfers from character to character as they meet with conflict.

10. Combine Unlike Things Together

What if elephants could breathe under the water? What if pigs could fly? What if Danny DeVito took a growth potion? What if's and unusual combinations sometime result in unique ideas for story.

"There's no use trying," said Alice. "One can't believe impossible things."

"I dare say you haven't much practice," said the Queen. "When I was your age, I always did it for half-an-hour a day. Why, sometimes I've believed as many as six impossible things before breakfast."—Lewis Carroll, *Through the Looking Glass* and *Alice in Wonderland*.

Getting ideas takes practice. Can you get six ideas today?

Pursuing Ideas

"Trust yourself. If it moves you, give it a chance. Don't hold back. *Monty Python* had a great working principle. They went with any idea one of them had, even if others didn't like it. They gave anything a chance to live on. Sometimes this resulted in a failed skit, but other times the results were completely unexpected and fantastic. If they had held back during early conceptualizing, they wouldn't have reached the unusual peaks they reached."—Larry Weinberg [6]

In short, you are searching for the *best* way to tell your story. Planning your animation takes as much time, rigor, and engagement (fun and frustration) as it takes to animate it. Progress is made over time and with investigation. Try to defer judgment until you play out your ideas a little bit.

Because we are people, and stories are about people, and we draw from our own experiences, dreams, and observations, frequently our first ideas have characters that are people and situations that initially are better for live action than animation. You have to play with these ideas and find exaggeration, metaphor, analogies that push the idea outside the boundaries of live action or communicate what you want to say in another form.

There are some tools we use to do this: research, brainstorming, condensation, and displacement. These are not isolated tools, but you move back and forth between them as you develop story.

Research

We use research to gather information. And there are three forms of research that you can employ to learn more about the content you need to produce.

1. Factual Research

Once you have your characters, conflict, and location, there will be many things that you just don't know. What do you know about medieval dragons or being lost at sea? This kind of research includes the mechanics of how something works, the architecture, costuming, or products of a particular era (what did a Coke bottle look like in 1962?); the cultural influences on your character or even what film, photography, advertising, and art look like in the time period or genre of your film. When Brad Bird made *The Iron Giant*, he filmed it in CinemaScope because that was the film ratio that was used in the 1950s, the time period of the story. He believed that using a film ratio from the time period of the story helped support the story itself. [7] Factual research can be an incredibly inspiring tool that can lead you to all types of potential for conflict and change. Change may lead to more research. Understanding the parameters of your content is important because out there, in your audience, someone knows your topic really well, and if you pass this off as "just animation," you will break the suspension of disbelief for someone in your audience.

2. Observational Research

We have already covered the fact that observation is one of an animator's greatest tools. You can learn a lot by watching. If you need to animate a lizard, get one. Watch it. Time the pacing of its movements. Record how it shifts weight when it walks, climbs, or twitches its tail. What else can you learn about it? How does it eat, sleep, and socialize? Observation can help you discover the essence of your character, location, or situation.

3. Experiential Research

This type of research is the most fun because you get to *do* things. When Pixar was making *Finding Nemo*, John Lasseter had all of the animators go scuba diving. It was his belief that they could not accurately animate an entire movie underwater unless they had experienced it. It is an entirely different thing to feel the resistance of the water, see the diffusion of the light, and actually swim with the fishes than to read about them or look at pictures. [8]

Experiential research is also where you act out what your character has to do. It is not enough to think about or observe an action. You need to get on your feet and *do* that action. Try it. Feel the force, weight, and pacing of the movement. Sometimes, you will have to animate a character or creature that moves very differently from the way you do, that has a very different weight, force, and attitude from yours. A great exercise is to follow people with a very different build and attitude from your own. Try to walk in their shoes—literally. Mirror their gait, the tilt of their head, the angle of their shoulders, the turn of their foot, the swing of their arms, and the angle of their hips. You will learn a lot about them from how they move as opposed to how *you* move.

Brainstorming

Most creativity texts will direct you to be uninhibited when you brainstorm. Anything goes. Play "What if?" extensively. To some degree, this is true. But, when developing story, you may get there faster if you work within some defined parameters:

- Define the time period and genre of your piece. Is it a horror, mystery, comedy, action-adventure, western, sci-fi, film noir, and so forth, and when does it take place?

- Cast and re-cast your characters until you find the right personality.

- List the attributes of your characters, what they do and where they do it. Attributes are all of the details you need to include in your visuals. Look at this sentence: The owner chased his dog through the crowded street. Clear enough. Until you go to draw it. What does the owner look like? How exactly does he "chase"? Does he run, hobble, cavort? What is the breed of dog? And who or what is populating the street? Is it a parade? A marketplace? A mob of Wall Street traders?

- Find metaphors. A metaphor is something that takes the place of something else. A woman on the prowl becomes a lion. A child at play becomes a small monkey. A methodical engineer becomes a robot. And they become something else because that "something" is closer to the actual essence of the character than the default package (human) in which you find it.

Brainstorm and share your ideas with others. Your piece will make sense to you because you made it. That doesn't mean it makes sense to others—and remember, stories are meant to be told to other people. Kick around your ideas. More minds make for more ideas.

Condensation

What if your idea has too many characters, events, or locations? Do you automatically abandon it? No. It may be that when you understand the essence of the story, it is possible to condense armies into a single soldier or a journey around the world into a walk around the block. Let's play "What if?" and condense one of our bigger stories, *Noggin*.

Let's say that this was your idea for a story but you either didn't have or didn't want other animators to collaborate with. Could you tell this story with two characters?

First, we need to determine what *Noggin* is really about. What is the concept of the piece?

Possible concepts that are within a standard deviation may be:

- Mutations save the species.
- Sometimes your differences are your strongest assets.
- Survival of the fittest.

Premise: Noggin, a prehistoric caveman, lives in conflict with the Bellyfaces who don't appreciate how his differences complicate their lives. Noggin's differences are what save him.

Without the introduction, we assume that Noggin is the first man, a mutation, living with Bellyfaces who ostracize him for his differences—a head that sits above the shoulders. He scares off prey because his head sticks out above the standard methods of camouflage, and his head smothers fire, which they worship, when he bows before it. The Bellyfaces decide that his head must go. But it is storming. And when a great flood comes, Noggin is the only creature who has his head above the water.

***Noggin*, directed by Alex Cannon, Brigham Young University**

The Bellyfaces are essentially all the same, so we could condense them into one character. Then populate the environment with symbols or images of the Bellyfaces, so your audience knows that Bellyfaces dominate the region. And we could probably do it all in and around the camp.

Noggin, **directed by Alex Cannon, Brigham Young University**

So we have two characters and one location. But we still have a long traditional intro, a quadruped deer, and a flood. Cut the intro. And the flood, the way it is staged and handled is probably okay. The deer is a problem. You have to model, rig, and animate a deer for just a few seconds of screen time. Maybe it could be a gopher that pops its head out of a hole. Better. The "prey" is swappable for feasibility without hurting the idea or action.

Displacement

Displacement means to change or displace to another viewpoint or context of a piece while maintaining the same story. When beginning to work ideas, look at all of the characters and toys at your disposal. Try telling the story through each of them individually and see what happens.

Poor Bogo is a story about a conflict between a father and his small daughter. The father wants his daughter to go to sleep and she wants to continue to tell a favorite bedtime story. Initially, this is an idea that would *seem* to be better for live action. You could caricature the players and stylize the room, and exaggerate the antics of the child and the sheer exhaustion of the father and this might suffice for animation well enough. But Thelvin Cabezas did a brilliant thing. He displaced the story to the object that was between the father and the child—the bedtime story.

Poor Bogo, by Thelvin Cabezas, Ringling College of Art and Design

This turns *Poor Bogo* into a more complex piece. The conflict is character against character. The child wants to stay awake and expand on the story of *Bogo*. This conflict is negotiated as the audience watches the child's imagination and the continuing story of *Bogo*. We have a story within a story.

Bogo is the hero of the child's story. He is in pursuit of candy. His conflict is twofold. He is in conflict with his environments. They pose physical obstacles to successfully gathering candy: treasure chests, ice cubes, and falling stars. He is also in conflict with the father. The father uses logic to dispel the obstacles just before Bogo can get the candy. And when the obstacles disappear, so does the candy. This has an emotional effect on Bogo and he relies on the child to infuse his goal with continued situations and hope.

By displacing the conflict between the father and child to the imaginary story, the artist allows the audience an insight into the much richer world of the child. Each time the father dispels the illusion with logic, Bogo expresses disappointment and we, too, are afraid that the story is over.

The main characters, father and child, do not have an arc to learn or experience an adrenaline moment. However, poor Bogo does. Remember the time I found a treasure chest? Remember the time there was an ice cube in the desert and when candy fell from the sky? Remember that there won't be any more adventures until another night (. . . and remember I never got to eat my candy!). Poor Bogo.

Summary

Before you start looking for ideas, know the rules of the animation playground:

- Story Is King
- Keep It Simple
- Know Your Concept or Theme
- Avoid Cliché
- Create a Memorable Character
- Emotion Drives Action
- Show, Don't Tell
- Create Conflict
- Know Your Ending
- Entertain Your Audience
- Make Me Laugh
- Do Something You Like
- There Are No Rules

Getting ideas takes practice and hard work.

Ideas come from:

- Everywhere
- Concepts
- Characters
- Location
- Situation
- Experience

- Questions
- Observation
- Negotiation
- Newspapers
- Art
- Other Stories
- Competition
- Combination
- Thinking Impossible Things

Giving ideas form involves thinking through the possibilities.

Tools for pursuing ideas include:

- Research
- Brainstorming
- Condensation
- Displacement

Recommended Readings

1. Don Hahn, *Dancing Corndogs in the Night*.

2. Ollie Johnston and Frank Thomas, *Too Funny for Words: Disney's Greatest Sight Gags*.

3. Michael Rabiger, *Developing Story Ideas*.

4. James L. Adams, *Conceptual Blockbusting*.

5. Jack Ricchiuto, *Collaborative Creativity*.

Notes

[1] Ed Hooks, *Acting For Animators*, Heinemann Press, Portsmouth, NH, 2003, p. 116.

[2] Ed Hooks, *Acting For Animators*, Heinemann Press, Portsmouth, NH, 2003, p. 6.

[3] Sylvain Chomet, *The Triplets of Belleville: The Cartoon According to Director Sylvain Chomet*, by Michel Robin, Beatrice Bonifassi, Jean-Claude Donda, and Mari-Lou Gauthier, released by Sony Pictures, 2004.

[4] Ray Bradbury, "There Will Come Soft Rains," in *The Martian Chronicles*, Spectra; Grand Master edition, 1984, p. 166.

[5] Katherine Tanner, Florida Studio Theater, Acting Workshops for Animators Homework Assignment.

[6]Angie Jones and Jamie Oliff, *Thinking Animation: Bridging the Gap between 2D and CG*, Course Technology PTR; 1 edition, 2006, p. 116.

[7]Salon.com, *Arts and Entertainment Column: Iron without Irony*, August 1999. *http://www.salon .com/ent/col/srag/1999/08/05/bird/index.html*.

[8]Eric Bana, Nicholas Bird (II), Albert Brooks, and Willem Dafoe, *Finding Nemo, Collectors Edition: Making Nemo*, Pixar Animation Studios, released by Walt Disney Pictures, 2003.

Making the Animated Short: An Interview with Andrew Jimenez, Pixar Animation Studios

Andrew Jimenez went to San Diego State University. His first big break was on *The Iron Giant* after which he moved to Sony Pictures to work on the first Spider-Man movie as a story reel editor and storyboard artist. That job led to a move to Pixar with Brad Bird to be a co-director of photography on *The Incredibles.* Most recently, Andrew, along with Mark Andrews, directed the Academy Award–nominated short, *One Man Band.*

***One Man Band,* directed by Andrew Jimenez and Mark Andrews, Pixar Animation Studios**

Q: What makes a good story for an animated short?

Andrew: Feature films and shorts are two completely different types of stories. When Mark Andrews and I were trying to come up with the idea for *One Man Band*, even when we were considering very un-fleshed-out ideas, it was clear that, OK, this idea belongs in a feature film and then this idea belongs in a short film.

It's a strange analogy to make, but a good short film is like a good joke. It has a great setup, gets to the point, and pays off right away. And it doesn't demand too much in terms of where the story has to go. It gets to the idea right away. You get it. Even if it takes you somewhere different from what you expected, it gets *there* right away, too. It's just very simple. And it's about one idea. It can have multiple characters, but it has to be very clear, because in 3 or 5 minutes you don't have time to really develop all these side stories and other plot lines.

To use the "joke" analogy again, if my timing isn't perfect and I go on a little bit too long, I can ruin it. I also think it's almost a little bit harder to tell a short film story, because you don't have the luxury to develop anything deeply, but yet it should be as meaningful.

It's funny because so many short films aren't short anymore. I think the biggest pitfall is that they are always the first act of a feature film, or they seem to be used as a vehicle for: "I'm just making this part of my bigger idea, but I'm using this to sell it." I'm always disappointed when I find out a short film has done that, because it ignores what is so wonderful about making short films.

Q: When you're building the story, how do you stay focused on one idea?

Andrew: One of the most important parts is the pitch. When your students or any new storyteller tells somebody else the idea, whoever is listening and/or the person pitching should really pay attention to how he or she is pitching.

I'll use *One Man Band* as an example:

There's a guy on a corner, and he's playing music. He's pretty good, but not really that good, and there is another musician that he is going to battle, musically. That's the story. That's it. The second I start pitching and telling, or describing events to the story that sort of breaks out of that little quad that this movie takes place in, that's the point where I start to get a little worried. The entire pitch should never break from that initial setup.

I think you should really be able to pitch your idea in 15 seconds. Even in *One Man Band*, the film never really breaks out away from what's presented in the first 15 seconds of the movie.

And it gets back to the joke analogy, which is a silly analogy, but I think it really makes the point well.

If I'm telling a joke, every beat of the story has to be right on the spot. In the feature film I can wander a little bit, lose you a little bit, I have time to get you back, but in the short film, if I lose you, there is no time to get you back. In the short film, if I go one beat too long, I can ruin it.

For example, if I start setting up giving too much background and explaining too much, then you, as an audience, start getting bored, and by the time I get to the punch line, it's like, uh, OK, that wasn't funny because you gave me way too much information.

I keep using the analogy of telling a joke. That is not to say that a good short film has to be funny. It's just a way of illustrating how important timing is in the short film format.

Q: Is it hard to be funny?

Andrew: Yes, absolutely. I know if I'm really trying to be funny, then I should stop right there. Stories are just like people. The funniest people never really try to be funny, they're just really funny. And in story, the funniest stories come out of the situations.

In *One Man Band,* we never really tried to be funny, or tried gags. I think some of the funniest moments came out of story beats and really great animation because the situation was funny in an honest way and always character-based. We never really set out to make a funny film.

The only thing with *One Man Band* that we started with before we created the story was that we knew we wanted to tell a story about music. There was a theme about what people do with talent and how people view other people that may have more talent than they do. Humor came out of story development but we never tried to *do humor* before we even knew what our characters were doing in the story. It is what the characters do—the acting—that makes it funny. Of course their designs played a big part of that, too.

Everything comes out of story. Whether you try to be depressing, or sad, or funny, or humorous, or make a statement, I think the second you try to do that without arriving at that through your story, then it's kind of like telling your punch line before your joke.

Q: What was the hardest part of making *One Man Band*?

Andrew: For *One Man Band* the hardest thing—it's true for the features, too—was that after we got the green light just to come up with ideas (and we were so ecstatic about that) was to actually come up with the ideas.

There's no science to coming up with a story. You can't say, "All right go—come up with a story." So, Mark and I started having lunch every day. We started talking about things we had in common, things we liked, things we didn't like in other movies.

I had this book I called "The Idea Book," and I wrote down all the ideas we came up with, about 50. One of the common themes in all these little ideas was music—and competition. I have been an avid film score collector since I was a child and have always wanted to tell a story where music was our characters' voices.

So we started developing and working around that theme. That time was the hardest part of the entire production of *One Man Band*—really getting that theme through the progression of the story. Because if you don't have that locked down and perfect, no matter how good the CG is or the acting is, you're never going to save it.

Don't worry about your perfectly rendered sunset, and shading and modeling of the set. It's the characters and their story. People will forgive so much if they really believe and love your characters and your story. When *Andre and Wally B.* was shown at Siggraph for the first time many years ago, most people in the audience didn't realize it wasn't finished because they were so involved in the characters.

Q: What advice do you give to animators making their first short?

Andrew: My advice would be: don't overcomplicate it. Just find one idea that you want to tell, stick with that, and trust it. If it's not working ask yourself why. Don't think you have to pile a bunch of other stuff on top of it to make it work and make it longer. Students, especially, will pack so much stuff into the film to try to show what they can do and to make *the* amazing film. I know I learned so much more by making several shorter films in the span of a year instead of making only one gigantic opus.

I know at Pixar, when we look at other short films, the thing we respond to the most is a short, simple idea that grabs us, that we get to react to it, and then it lets us go.

Chapter 3

Acting: Exploring the Human Condition

The Songs of Jacques Brel, **Photo Courtesy of Florida Studio Theatre and**
The Kite **by Gwynne Olson-Wheeler**

Animators are actors. They create every nuance of a performance and breathe life into each character that they animate. The very essence of their craft embodies the root of the word animation—*anima*, which in Latin means breath of life. Kathy Altieri, Production Designer at DreamWorks Feature Animation, explains it this way:

When you're an artist, you have to feel and experience what you're trying to draw.

For example, if I'm drawing a figure, I need to feel the weight of her hip on the chair. I need to feel the pull of her waist as she twists. It has nothing to do with the external shape; it has to do with sympathy for what the model is doing and feeling and how that affects the line that comes out of my hand.

In animation, it's all about getting the audience to feel a certain way. We do this in every department, through music, lighting, color, and line. The animator has us in his powerful grip. If he can *Feel* what his character is feeling, he will communicate that through even the smallest movements his character performs. He quite literally becomes the actor portraying the role. The more fluent he becomes at acting himself, the better his character will communicate to us, the audience, and the more we will feel what we are supposed to feel at any given moment in the film.

An actor is trained to "feel what the character is feeling," and then authentically convey that through the character's expressions and gestures. It is this authenticity that separates good actors from the rest, and good animators from the mediocre. Instead of merely *representing* emotion by playing an idea of "fear," "happy," or "'sad," as a new or amateur actor might, the good actor *recreates* the emotional feeling. Like an actor, in this chapter you will study the art of acting. You will learn a simple acting technique that will teach you:

- How to build a character by:
  - Developing the *inner* life—the emotional state of being that is conveyed through expression and gesture
    - How thought creates emotion
    - How emotion creates gesture
  - Developing the *outer* life
    - How a character is further defined in the scene by specifically identifying the goals, tactics, and actions

Additionally, by studying the art of acting you will learn to:

- Use the tools of *emotional recall* and *empathy* to "get inside" your character and avoid creating cliché expressions and gestures

- Understand and create characters that are different from you, the animator

Ultimately, by learning and using an acting technique during the animation process, you will be able to create believable characters that capture and move your audience during every moment of your film.

Acting I: Building Character

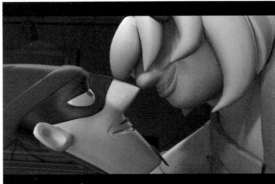

Prelude to a Kiss, **Photo Courtesy of Florida Studio Theatre;** *The Dancing Thief* **by Meng Vue**

At the turn of the 20th century, Russian actor Constantin Stanislavski—the father of modern acting—discovered how an actor could access human emotion and express it onstage to an audience. He found that when preparing to build a character, one must first develop the *inner life*—the emotions, thoughts, and gestures—that makes that specific character become alive and real to the audience. Therefore, Stanislavski developed a method, called the *Theory of Psycho-Physical Action*, through which an actor could create the inner life, or emotional core, of any character by employing two elements:

- The Psychological Mind
  - The images in our brains that create emotion
- The Physical Body
  - The gestures and movements that reflect the images in the psychological mind

By utilizing these two elements you will be able to think, feel, and move like your character; and eventually, you will be able to make stronger, more emotionally active choices that reveal the character's development in your story.

We will begin the actor training process with exercises that focus on each element separately. We will then put the two elements—Psychological Mind and Physical Body—together, for then you will see why and how both must be present to create authentic characters.

Exploring the Psychological Process

Proof, Photo Courtesy of Florida Studio Theatre *Fox Cry* **by Gary Schumer**

Images in the mind create emotion. Imagine that at any moment of the day there is a film in your mind that continuously runs and creates pictures. These pictures, in turn, create emotion.

Example #1:

You are driving your car thinking about an incident that made you angry. As you drive, you repeat the incident over and over in your mind, and your emotion builds. Finally, by the time you arrive at your destination and get out of the car, you are furious!

It is the replaying of the incident, or the reel of film, in your mind that creates the flow of emotion. This process of replaying mental pictures of a past incident is called *emotional recall.*

Example #2:

You are having an uneventful coffee date with friends, and you unexpectedly find yourself daydreaming about someone you will see later that night. Suddenly, you are flooded with good feelings that transport you out of the situation.

These positive feelings come from *thinking* about that person. This process of imagining an unknown experience is called *empathy*. Like emotional recall, mental pictures or thoughts bring about empathy. These pictures in the mind are called *images*. Throughout the day we have a private inner world of images that determine our emotional state, and for an actor, they are the keys that unlock what a character is feeling in a specific situation.

Acting Technique

Element I: Exploring Emotion

You will need a simple chair and a quiet room. Afterwards, you can record your observations.

Exercise A—Love: Sit in a chair and make yourself comfortable. Close your eyes and imagine someone you love. Pick an image of that person. You may use:

- *Emotional Recall*: the memory of a loved one
- *Empathy*: an imagined future love

Think of her specifically: the color of her hair, the way her lip curves, something she has said to you, and when you last saw her. Let the images get deeper within you. Let them flow. The images should create a flood of feelings for this person whom you love. Observe these feelings.

Observe:

How do these feelings move through your body?

How does your heart feel?

Does your pulse quicken?

How does your face change?

How does this feeling affect your hands? Your feet?

Do these feelings relax you?

Sample:

Feeling	Image	Sensations
Love	Grandmother	Flood of warmth, heart muscles relaxed

Record your impressions.

Feeling	Image	Sensations
Love		

Repeat this exercise with the "love" of another person—a Grandfather, a child, a sister. How do the feelings change or intensify within your body?

Exercise B—Anger: Sit in a chair and make yourself comfortable. Close your eyes and imagine someone you have a conflict with. Just as in Exercise A, think of him specifically until you have a flood of feelings.

Observe:

How do these feelings move through your body?

How does your heart feel? (Hurt or tight?)

Does your pulse quicken?

How does your face change?

How does this feeling affect your hands? Your feet?

Do these feelings make you feel constricted?

Record your impressions.

Feeling	Image	Sensations
Anger		

Trying out other feelings:

Experiment with different feelings. There are many kinds of loneliness, many kinds of joy. The good actor is like a violin or a painter—he can play an infinite number of notes or combine an array of colors to achieve a fresh, authentic interpretation. By utilizing this exercise, you will learn to incorporate authentic emotion in your work and develop the discerning eye to see it in others.

Record your impressions and remember to be specific with your images.

ACTING NOTEBOOK FOR ANIMATORS		
Feeling	Image	Sensations
Love		
Anger		
Loneliness		
Jealousy		
Embarrassment		
Fear		

The Actor Trap #1: What Not to Do!

Cliché Sad and Emotionally Filled Sad with actress Christianne Greiert, Photos by Maria Lyle

New artists sometime show cliché emotions. For example, when asked to portray an emotion, they will smile widely to show happy or they will frown deeply to show sad. Using overly simplified external expressions that are crudely portrayed will not convey emotion. The result? A generic and empty character. Always infuse your character with authentic emotion.

Applying the Psychological Process to a Character

Grimmy by Mike Peters

You now know how to access an authentic feeling using emotional recall or empathy. Now, apply it to a character that you are developing. Whether the character is a vengeful chair, a rambunctious bull, or even Hamlet:

- Find the moment you want to express
- Use your acting technique to feel the corresponding emotion
- Observe how the emotion affects you
- Transpose this emotion to the character

For example, an actor is studying Hamlet. He knows that Hamlet is consumed by revenge due to the wrongful death of his father. However, the actor has never experienced the death of his own father. How does he emotionally connect to Hamlet? Instead of playing the amateur idea of Hamlet as a crazy madman, the actor looks at each moment in the play and identifies what Hamlet is feeling. Then, by using emotional recall and empathy, he chooses images from his own life so that he can relate to the character's specific emotional moments. Thus, he can begin to fathom the depth of Hamlet's pain.

Remember—be *specific* to the moment that you want to express.

- Amateurs—project generalized feelings that do not correspond to the moment
- Trained Professionals—convey feelings specific to the moment

Exploring the Physical Gesture

Ethel Waters: His Eye Is on the Sparrow, Photo Courtesy of Florida Studio Theatre;
A Great Big Robot from Outer Space Ate My Homework by Mark Shira

The psycho-physical technique: the body is the counterpart of the mind. Whether we are gently combing our hair or slamming a door, every physical gesture we express *reflects* our emotional state. For example, a first-time offender on trial who is trying to appear calm but nervously taps her pencil reveals the truth of how worried and anxious she is. Whereas the physical expression of a hardened criminal who methodically taps his pencil, perhaps biding time as he awaits his expected sentence, reveals a different emotional state. In turn, a first-time father who is trying to appear calm while nervously tapping his pencil in a hospital waiting room, is also anxious but in a completely different way. Yet in all instances, the physical gesture of tapping the pencil is colored by the emotional state of the character. The great Charlie Chaplin knew and embodied this principle whether he was holding out a flower for his love or stepping out of the way from being run over by a car. Emotion and physicality are intertwined, for one cannot exist without the other.

Emotion, like a current of electricity, informs every gesture—every movement of the body. Using what we have learned in "images," you will now take part in exercises designed to explore how emotion *influences* the body. You will need a chair and a book.

Acting Technique

Element II: Exploring Physicality

Exercise A—Love: Sit in a chair and make yourself comfortable. Hold the book. Using emotional recall or empathy, select an image of someone you love. Again, think of her specifically: the color of her hair, the way her lip curves, something she has said to you, and when you last saw her. Let the images get deeper within you. Let them flow. The images should create a flood of feelings for this person. Observe these feelings.

Observe yourself while sitting in the chair.

How does your body feel in that chair? (Languid, relaxed, comfortable?)

Pick a gesture: Curl your hair, tap your foot, or twist a necklace.

Explore the tension in your muscles. Observe the tempo of your tapping.

Now, rise and walk across the room, carrying the book with you.

Explore how these feelings inform how you carry the book.

Is the book held closely? Gingerly?

Observe your walk.

How do you walk? Long strides or short? Dreamy or slow?

Observe how relaxed or excited you are.

Sample:

Feeling	Image	Sensations	Physical Gestures
Love	Grandmother	I feel a flood of warmth; heart muscles relaxed.	I hold the book tenderly, slowly leafing through the pages.

Record your impressions:

Feeling	Image	Sensations	Physical Gestures
Love			

Exercise B—Anger: Sit in a chair and make yourself comfortable. Hold the book. Using emotional recall or empathy, think of an image that makes you angry. When you have a flood of feelings, begin to observe your physicality.

Observe yourself while sitting in the chair.

How tense is your body?

Pick a gesture: Curl your hair, tap your foot, or flip the pages in the book.

Explore the tension in your muscles. Observe the tempo of the tapping.

How does it differ from love? Does the tap change into a stomp?

Observe how you hold the book.

 Do you grip it?

 What do your fingers feel like?

Now, rise and walk across the room with the book.

Observe how the feelings of anger inform how you carry the book.

 Is the book held closely?

 Do you throw the book down?

Observe your walk.

 How do you walk? Long strides or short? What is the tempo?

Observe your posture.

 Is it tense? Slumped?

Record your impressions.

Feeling	Image	Sensations	Physical Gestures
Anger			

Trying out other physicalities:

Try out other movements and gestures. As we discussed, there are many kinds of feelings and each informs the body in a different way. Observe yourself in your daily life. Observe your mood and how it is reflected in your gestures at the checkout counter, walking to class, or taking a test. By incorporating this exercise, you will learn to inform the physical characters you create with the specific emotional reality of their situation.

Try sitting at your desk and writing a letter to someone you are:
 Jealous about
 Mad at
 Hurt by
 Worried for

Try pacing in the doctor's office waiting room and you are:
 Bored
 Interested
 Frustrated

Record your impressions and remember to be specific with your images.

ACTING NOTEBOOK FOR ANIMATORS			
Feeling	Image	Sensations	Physical Gestures
Love			
Anger			
Loneliness			
Jealousy			
Embarrassment			
Fear			

Actor Trap #2: Only Using One Element Results in False Acting

Image without a Gesture **Gesture without an Image** **Image and Gesture**

Photos by Adam D. Martens with actress Christianne Greiert

Often new actors will mistakenly use only one element, either psychological or physical, which will result in "false" acting. They will portray an emotion without any physicality or show a physical gesture without emotion. For example, if a director instructs a student to "act scared," and then he or she chooses to act "scared" by shaking the body nervously and bugging out the eyes, the performance will be a cliché of acting—an empty shell. (This should not be confused with comic caricature.) Again, bad actors *represent* emotion. Good actors know how to incorporate the psycho-physical technique and *recreate authentic* characters using *emotion* and *gesture*.

A Note about Character

In Chapter 4, you will begin working intensively with *character*. The character design is a shell that must be informed by many elements including education, culture, upbringing, personality, age, gender, and more. Actors call this the *mask*. More importantly, remember that the emotional state is *filtered* through this shell (mask) of character. Therefore, how characters will react in a given situation is determined by their personal traits and emotions. For example, if a character is frightened, it will be expressed differently if the character is:

- A 17th century French Countess who may have "learned emotions" and will not reveal anything that is not acceptable. Even her gestures are prescribed.

- A 20th century immigrant teen in Miami.

- A 21st century teenager who tries to look "cool" and be aloof because she is afraid to show any real feelings.

Applying the Physical Process to a Character

Grimmy by Mike Peters

You now know how to access an authentic physicality that is connected to your emotions. Now, apply it to a character that you are developing. Whether the character is a princess, a teapot, or even Ophelia:

- Find the moment you want to express
- Use your acting technique to feel the corresponding emotion
- Apply that emotion to your body
- Transpose the psycho-physical knowledge to the character

For example, an actress is studying Ophelia. She knows that Ophelia is consumed by the deaths of her father and brother, Polonius and Laertes. However, the actress has never experienced death of this magnitude. In one particular scene, Ophelia is throwing imaginary flowers on her father's grave. How does the actress emotionally connect to Ophelia doing this action? Instead of playing the amateur idea of Ophelia as a crazy young girl (running around wide-eyed), the actress looks at each moment in the play and identifies what Ophelia is feeling. In this specific moment, the actress discovers that Ophelia is sad as she remembers her father. She then explores how this specific emotion moves through her body and finds her movement to be languid and deliberate because she is reflecting on this loss. Thus, she throws the flowers slowly and deliberately onto the grave.

Acting II: Exploring Scene Work

"Words are like toy boats on the water."

—Sonia Moore

Metamorphosis, **Photo Courtesy of Florida Studio Theatre;** *Catch* **by Chris Perry**

The essential elements of a scene in acting are as follows: objective, intentions, and *actions.* Now that we have explored how to create emotion and gesture in a character, we will begin to place that character in a *scene.* In *animation* you use the words *goal, tactics,* and *actions.*

- The *objective/goal* is what the character wants.
- The *intentions/tactics* are the different ploys the character uses to achieve the objective.
- The *actions* are the physical choices the character uses in concert with the intentions.

We only need to look at life around us to understand scene work. We live in dialogue, goals, and actions every day. For example, suppose Ashley and Adam are having a conversation and Joe enters the room. Ashley feels Joe is intruding and wants him to leave. Her *goal* is to convince Joe to leave the room. However, she will use different *tactics* to achieve her goal. At first, Ashley may *sweet talk* Joe. "Sweetie, would you mind if I asked you to step outside and get something for me?" If he leaves, she has achieved her goal and the scene is over. However, let's say Joe doesn't leave. Now, Ashley's goal is the same, but she will change her tactic. This time she will pull him aside (action) and *implore* him. "Sweetie, please, would you get a drink for me, please?" And if this doesn't work, she might just go for a third tactic and *threaten* him. "You better leave now!" And if Joe still doesn't leave? Ashley will commit to an *action* and go to the phone to call the police. She has used three different ways (tactics) to get Joe to leave, and, if he does, she reaches resolution.

The Actor Notebook for the scene would read as follows:

Objective/Goal	To make Joe leave the room.
Intentions/Tactics	Ask. Implore. Threaten.
Actions	Pull Joe aside. Go to the phone to call the police.

Keep in mind that the *tactics you choose are a reflection of the character.* For instance, the tactics in the previous scene change if:

- Ashley is a confident, headstrong 19-year-old girl
- Ashley is a quiet, shy, and needy person

The use of these essential elements *gives your scene purpose and heightens the conflict.* Occasionally, characters are in accord and struggle for the same goal, just as when Woody and the toys band together to save Buzz. On the other hand, when the Queen seduced Snow White into eating the poisoned apple, each character was struggling for something different and was clearly at odds. Every film, play, or animated short uses scenes just like this to tell a story and thereby builds the conflict to reach a dynamic conclusion—the resolution.

Developing Intentions and Objectives in the Dialogue and Action

The dialogue of the characters must be imbued with the character's objectives and intentions. As the great acting teacher Sonia Moore said, "The words are like toy boats on the water." Think of every important moment in your life. Did the words ever convey the depth of your feelings? Think of the final goodbye you said to a friend or your first break-up. Underneath the words are the emotional currents—the intentions, needs, goals, and desires, as expressed through the silent actions of the characters. One of the delights of the animated short is the minimal use of language. Yet, while the dialogue of a scene is usually simple, it is important to remember that the words only become powerful when they are forged with authentic emotions.

The goals and intentions/tactics give the language its meaning and context. To learn about how an intention clarifies the language, let's look at this sample scene with the assigned characters of A and B. You can view this work on the companion DVD titled *Acting: Exploring the Human Condition*, but first read the scene without any inflection.

A. Hi.

B. Hi.

A. How are you?

B. Ok.

A. Really?

B. Yeah.

A. Well, I'll call you later.

B. Bye.

A. Bye.

At first glance, this is a "nonsense" scene. It doesn't really make sense, yet it feels slightly familiar because of the usage of common conversational words such as "Hi" and "Bye." However, we don't have any context for the scene so we don't really know what the characters are talking about.

Impose an objective/goal on the scene to create meaning. Let's say that Partner A's objective is to make up with Partner B. Partner A is in love with Partner B. They had a fight. Partner A wants to make up and Partner B does too. Now, using what you learned about emotional recall or empathy, read the scene out loud or with a partner.

Objective #1: To make up.

Result: You can probably feel how emotionally connected the two characters are. We all have felt this. The two characters are in agreement and a resolution is reached.

Write down your result.

Read the scene again and change the objectives.

- Partner A will choose *to make up.*
- Partner B will choose *to reject.*

Notice how the change in Partner B's objective will affect the whole tenor of the script. Let's call this scene "The Break-Up."

Objective #2: Partner A's objective is to make up. Partner B's objective is to reject the offer.

Result: You will hear a completely different reading of the same scene as the objectives and intentions infuse the text with the emotional truth of the relationships. (See the DVD.)

Write down your result.

Improvisation

Mark Shira and his character from *A Great Big Robot from Outer Space Ate My Homework*

"I can't stress enough how acting out the scenes and filming myself on a web cam helped . . . . it is so helpful in getting both the broad strokes as well as subtleties of performance."

—Mark Shira

"The creation of something new is not accomplished by the intellect but by the play instinct."

—Carl Jung

Improvisation is unscripted, uninhibited play to discover something "new." When actors need to find the reality of a scene, explore a character's motivation, work out an ending, or even when they are "stuck," they rely on improvisation. Improvising a scene helps you get at its heart, for it can move you beyond the current limits of your imagination into new territory. Also, by freeing themselves from restrictions in the script and playing the intentions and actions, the actor will discover unique gestures and movement choices that are particular to their character. Steve Smith, director of the Big Apple Circus, author, and lecturer says, "I use improvisation all the time. It gives adults permission to play; to get into the sandbox and discover and uncover the 6-year-old inside of them—the innocence and naiveté that is the fountainhead of creativity. It is the truth."

- When improvising, remember to use your objectives, intentions, and actions.
- Let yourself be unedited as you explore the story. Kick. Stomp the floor. Giggle too loud. Cry. Experience rage. You can only discover something new if you move past your limits.
- Remember that self-consciousness is antithetical to the creative process. If you get embarrassed (like Mark Shira), stop for a moment and record that process as an emotional recall memory in your Actor Notebook.

The Iconic Moment

Study of Degas' Absinthe **by Gary Schumer;** *Fantasia Taurina* **by Alejandra Pérez Gonzalez**

The iconic moments are the important storytelling images in the scene. They are emotionally heightened because they are at once natural and familiar to the audience. They are moments that lift the audience out of the ordinary and say, "Life is important. Each moment is important. Look." We participate in these moments every day of our lives. We only have to look around us. It is:

- The mother brushing her child's hair
- A young son glancing back at his father before he leaves home for the first time
- Lovers parting and couples waving hello
- The greeting of long lost brothers
- A mother carrying her dead child in war
- The teen behind the wheel of his first car

We also see iconic moments in film, animation, and art. Familiar images such as:

- Rafiki holding up a newborn babe
- Bambi screaming for his mother
- Shrek and Donkey sitting under the moon
- A woman alone at a table in Degas' *Absinthe*

The *iconic moments* in the following scene can be viewed on the DVD titled *Acting: Exploring the Human Condition*. The actors have improvised the scene that we called "The Break-Up." Look closely at the scene and find their iconic moments. We have chosen seven. They are as follows:

1. The Anticipation

2. The Look

3. The First Attempt at Reconciliation

4. The Second Attempt at Reconciliation

5. The Rejection

6. The Crisis

7. The Resolution with actors Adam Ratner and Katherine Michelle Tanner

Choosing the iconic moments is important to your story because:

- You identify what is necessary and important to the scene
- You condense the story to a feasible time period
- You identify the *must-have* images for the audience

Improvise your scene and choose your iconic moments. When you complete your scene concept, improvise it fully and freely many times over. Remember:

- Use goals, tactics, and actions that are forged with the emotional reality of the scene
- The scene will most likely be long and formless
- Step back and look at the scene as an observer
- Identify the iconic moments: the important storytelling images

Soon you will find the shape of your animated short and be able to move it from a generic, free-form story to the artfulness of a universal tale.

In Conclusion

Acting is truth—the specific emotions of a character in the moment that are honest and true. Whether your character is a penguin, a rat, a tomato, or a prince, he/she/it is imbued with *anima*—the breath of life of the human condition. Through the study of acting, animators can access important tools to breathe a vital emotional and physical dimension into their characters.

***The Kite* by Gwynne Olson-Wheeler**

First, by employing the Stanislavski technique of psycho-physical action we learned that:

- Images create emotion
- The physical body—its movement and gesture—is a reflection of one's inner feelings and emotion

Moreover, in order to build an authentic character we must use the acting technique to discover:

- How a character truly *feels* moment to moment
- How a character *moves* moment to moment

Thus, we come to the realization that both the mind and body must be employed to make a character come alive. And remember, a cliché gesture is just a generic rendition of an emotion that does not really express the character's feelings and does not generate empathy from the audience.

Secondly, the essential elements for scenes are as follows:

- Goals
- Tactics
- Actions
- Resolution

The characters must want something with their heart and soul. They then work to get it by using their tactics until there is a resolution.

Finally, improvisation will help you get on your feet, think outside of the box, and discover new ways that a character might behave. And, as a finishing touch, the iconic moments will shape the piece so that it is accessible and familiar to the audience.

Acting is truth. It is the exploration of the human condition in all its authentic joys and sorrows. By learning the art of acting your characters will better "communicate to us, the audience, and the more we will feel what we are supposed to feel at any given moment in the film."

Summary

- Capture "true" emotion that is authentic and specific to the moment.
- Use the psycho-physical technique.
- Psychological process: Images in the mind create emotion. Use emotional recall and empathy to remember a personal experience or find an emotional connection to others by asking: "What if . . .?"
- Physical gestures inform the audience of the character's emotional state.

- Avoid cliché: Generalized emotion that is not specific to the moment robs your characters of emotional truth.

- Mask/Shell: Decisions regarding culture, upbringing, or personality that will determine how much of a character's emotional core is revealed.

- Scene work involves three essential elements: objectives, intentions, and actions.

- Dialogue must be imbued with the character's objectives and intentions.

- Improvisation is unscripted, uninhibited play to discover something new.

- Iconic moments are the important storytelling images in the scene.

- Acting is truth: The portrayal of a character that is true to the depth of the emotional reality he or she is trying to express.

Recommended Readings

Hooks, Ed. *Acting for Animators, Revised Edition: A Complete Guide to Performance in Animation.*

Johnstone, Keith. *Improv for Storytellers.*

McGaw, Charles. *Acting Is Believing: A Basic Method.*

Moore, Sonia. *Training an Actor: The Stanislavski System in Class.*

Spolin, Viola. *Improvisation for the Theatre.*

Stanislavski, Constantin. *An Actor Prepares.* New York: Theatre Arts Books, 1989.

Visual Design: Interviews with Kendal Cronkhite and Kathy Altieri, DreamWorks Feature Animation

Kendal Cronkhite graduated from Art Center College of Design in Pasadena, California, with a major in illustration. After working for magazines and newspapers, a former instructor recommended her for work on *Tim Burton's The Nightmare Before Christmas*. Kendal then art directed on *James and the Giant Peach* before going to DreamWorks to art direct on *Antz*. She was production designer for *Madagascar* and is now production designer for *Madagascar: The Crate Escape*.

Q: Some animation studios seem to have an identifiable style or "look" to all their films while DreamWorks seems to develop a new look or style for each film. Do you agree this is true? And could you talk a little bit about how content influences design?

Kendal: It's absolutely true. It's a standard that we try to hold to studiowide. I remember sitting down with the *Antz* directors and producers, and saying, "All right, do you want us to design for the computer?" And they said, "Absolutely not, we want you to design what's right for our story and we'll figure out how to make it technically later."

By designing what is right, visually, for the story, we end up pushing the technology. We don't want to do what's been done before; we don't want to repeat ourselves. It's more exciting, and it's more interesting creatively for all of us. And it kind of moves us into the future.

Q: How do you begin to come up with the design for the film?

Kendal: We read the script, the treatment, and then break it down and start to design the movie that visually tells that particular story. I often start by doing the visual structure on the film. This is a visual map that follows the drama. I use line, shape, space, and color to enhance what's going on in our story. For example, if it's a movie about coming home again I may use circles as a design element throughout. If there are emotional highs and lows, I may enhance those moods with light and darkness. If it's a traveling film, I may choose to use deep space and focus. After this visual map is created, we go into each set and sequence in greater detail. We also look for the style for the film. Is it a comedy or drama? Is it a certain time period? All these questions are asked and answered visually.

I can take you through how Madagascar happened. Initially, what was really striking about the story was that it was a real New York–style comedy. The characters came across as real New Yorkers with a definite East Coast sense of humor. There was a lot of physicality to it.

In talking with the directors, we felt strongly that here was our chance actually to do something we had thought about before—to make a real 3D cartoon. It just seemed to suit it.

One of the first things we did was hire a character designer, Craig Kellman, whose strength has been to take retro 2D character styles and infuse them with a modern edge. He came from Cartoon Network and had designed characters for *Powerpuff Girls* and *Samurai Jack*.

He initially nailed down our four lead characters. They have a stylistic point of view that was based in the design of the 1950s and 1960s. A strong design element is contrast between straight edges and curves.

The humor in the design is in the pushed proportions. Alex the lion has a huge head on a really thin body. Gloria has a huge body with tiny hands and feet.

When you look at something that has those extreme proportions, it's funny and that was really important to the tone of our film. So we took those elements and then designed our world around them.

When you look at our world, everything is also designed with straights against curves and pushed proportions. It also has what we call a "whack" factor—sort of a cartoony design element. Let's say you had a building. You would never design a straight, linear-shaped building. You would do what we call "whack," which means you would angle the sides, the tops and windows off kilter to each other. Additionally, every leaf on every tree—all the vein patterns, the bark on the jungle trees—everything is stylized the same way.

In most other films, jungles have been mysterious, disorienting, claustrophobic, and for our film we couldn't have that. Our jungles needed to be cheery and fanciful and slightly childlike, because our characters were new to this environment—like children seeing it for the first time.

The director said, "Well what about Henri Rousseau? His jungles have that oversized, child-like, naive quality. They have primary colors everywhere." So, we combined Rousseau with our stylistic concept to get that childlike, beautiful, sweet jungle out of *Madagascar*.

Q: So, when you design, a lot of what you choose is based on the point of view of the characters in the story—what and how they would see things, correct?

Kendal: Yes. Try to put yourself in the character's shoes, and then move through the story. In *Madagascar*, we wanted the characters—in the moment they hit the beach—to feel like they were in a world unlike anything they had experienced before.

In New York, we tried to make everything feel very manmade. The plant life is very manicured and contained within metal chain-link fences because we also wanted the feeling of containment. Not trapped necessarily, but that our characters were contained within this atmosphere. So even when birds fly up, they can't get out of the surrounding cityscape. You never see them escape. We also took out the sun, moon, and stars, even though we have night and day. Everything is linear and straight. There are few curves in that world. We tried to strip all of nature *out*.

So when we hit Madagascar, it was all nature *in*. Madagascar is all about curves, the sun, the moon, the clouds, the stars, and the bounty of nature. We wanted the audience to have the same experience that our characters had when seeing Madagascar for the first time—complete awe.

These designs, then, are character-driven and that is very important.

Kathy Altieri has been working in the animation industry for more than 25 years. She began as a background painter in television animation and then went to Walt Disney

Feature Animation as a background painter and supervisor on *The Little Mermaid, Aladdin, The Lion King,* and *The Hunchback of Notre Dame.* At DreamWorks, she was an art director on the *Prince of Egypt,* and production designer on *Spirit: Stallion of the Cimarron, Over the Hedge,* and currently, *How to Train Your Dragon* (2009).

Hammy (Steve Carell) has no idea that he's about to be "booked" by a Trail Guide Gal in Dream-Works Animation's computer-animated comedy *Over the Hedge.* **Over the Hedge™ & © 2006 DreamWorks Animation LLC All Rights Reserved**

Q: Could you talk a little bit about how content influences design in *Over the Hedge*?

Kathy: There's no question that the scenarios in *Over the Hedge* could be happening, at least in some part, right now in our very own backyards, in real life. It's a film about how critters have learned to adapt to our enthusiastic development of the wilderness. Since the film is meant to reflect our lives and homes as they really are, the film's style is basically realistic. The homes are "set dressed" to look like our own backyards, complete with doggie toys and old lawn chairs, beat-up grass, and barbeques. The lighting and atmosphere are realistic; the homes are built in the computer to imitate the homes that are built in the Midwest.

In addition, one of our directors, Tim Johnson, felt that we have a strong emotional connection to the photographs we all have in our albums—so we re-created a similar lighting environment that we recognize in photographs. It has to do with the behavior of light in the lightest lights and darkest darks. The average viewer won't notice these choices, but they add to the feeling we were trying to create of familiarity, of home.

Q: You had some interesting copyright issues when it came to designing some of the elements of *Hedge* that, I think, beginning storytellers wouldn't consider. Could you talk about those considerations a little bit?

Kathy: You have to be really careful when you're working on a film that's set in a contemporary environment. Any product you use in your film that's recognizable from real life has to be carefully examined for possible copyright infringements. Any product you design or logo you make cannot bear any resemblance to the real product without first clearing it from the manufacturers themselves. In addition, any spoof of an existing product also has to be considered.

For example, we had girls in *Over the Hedge* delivering cookies door to door. Of course, these were originally meant to be Girl Scouts, but the Girl Scouts of America had objections to what we had "their" girls do in the film, basically smash a squirrel with a Girl Scout Handbook. Of course, this is a cartoon, and no squirrel was really hurt—but we completely understood their concern and went about designing our own fake girls' organization, the Trail Guide Gals. Every last detail of the Trail Guide Gals had to be passed through legal for clearance—the color and style of their uniform, their logo, the design of the handbook, the type of bow they had at their neck, even the name itself.

Q: Where does this type of thing come into play for young animators?

Kathy: In any creative undertaking, we all strive to be as original as possible. In doing so, it's really important to be aware of and respect copyright and trademark laws. Being a student or young professional does NOT exclude you from responsibility to this, so be aware that all of your work should be truly original and unique to you.

Closing: What are the important things to remember when designing a film?

Kendal Cronkhite: One of the most important things is that you're a filmmaker; you're not just an illustrator or a painter. So how a film turns out on the screen is the most important thing. Learn the process, and immerse yourself in the filmmaking. Learn about camera and camera composition, line and shape, space and light, and how it all comes together to create a strong cinematic point of view.

When you decide on a visual point of view for a film, the best way to get it across is to be consistent through every aspect of it, from the character design to the design of the world to every element that goes into that world, and it should work with the story and the tone of the story.

We start designing in art, but then it goes through many departments before it ends up on screen. From art to modeling to surfacing to lighting to animating, you have to make sure you are staying true to what is important in the design. So that when you get this image on screen and your characters are moving around in it, it says what you want it to say, throughout the movie.

There are a lot of voices and a lot of stress in the kitchen, and it gets hard to juggle it all. You have to feel pretty passionately about it, and stick to your guns. That can be challenging over a two- to three-year process. Have a strong point of view and see it through.

Chapter 4

Building Character and Location

Stories are about people. The people (toys, monsters, fish, aliens, cars, robots, etc.) are the characters through which the story is told. The story belongs to the character. Without a good character you don't have a story.

KuhFo, directed by Hannes Appell & Holger Wenzl, Filmakademie Baden-Wurttemberg, Germany

What Is a Good Character?

A good character is one that is both believable and memorable.

A believable character is an ordinary character (in relation to the world that he lives in) who finds himself in extraordinary circumstances and reacts to those circumstances truthfully.

A memorable character is visually appealing and has the ability to move an audience emotionally through the events of the story.

Appeal is dependent on the visual design of the character. Ollie Johnson and Frank Thomas originally coined the term *appeal* in their book, *The Illusion of Life*. To them, appeal meant that "your eye is drawn to a character and you appreciate what you are seeing." [1] You immediately identify with the character. The character can be beautiful or ugly, intricate or plain, good or bad. The character's appeal makes you want to watch him and find out more about him.

You learn more about a character as you progress through a story. An appealing design is complemented by a captivating personality. A good character is embedded with personality traits that an audience can identify with; ones that are strong and recognizable. These traits are constructed to either aid or impede the character in the pursuit of her goal. As you watch and get to know more about the character, she engages you. You begin to hope for the character's success or failure. At each event in the story, your emotional investment becomes greater.

A good character is one that is right for the story.

Character Profiles

A good character is also a character that you understand. Knowing your character well allows you to construct believable reactions to conflicts faced in the story. These reactions are what will move your audience through the story. To engage the audience, you need a fully developed character.

What does that mean? In films, there are many types of characters. There are main characters, supporting characters, opposing characters, minor characters, and extras. The term *flat* is often used to describe minor characters or extras. As an audience, we don't get to know them very well. They are singular in both function and emotion. Sometimes they are more like props used to move the story forward. Main characters are fully developed. We engage in them because they have a history complete with a full range of emotion, strengths, weaknesses, idiosyncrasies, and faults.

In feature films character development is called a *back story*. A back story is an extensive biography of the character. It includes everything from physical features, education, professional history, family, relationships, lifestyle, hobbies, sports, successes, failures, past diseases, disorders, strengths, weaknesses, fears, and phobias to a myriad of other traits.

For the short we just don't need to know that much. There is not much time, in the few minutes your film will last, for deep character development. Instead, your audience needs to know immediately who your character is and what he or she wants. As the animator, you need to know a bit more to progress the story. But what you need to know can be limited to a few major traits determined by the following definitive questions:

1. What is your character's ethical perspective? Ethics are the means by which we make decisions. Knowing—or assigning—an ethical baseline to your character will help you keep him consistent in the way that he approaches conflict. Paul Lester, author of Visual Communication, outlines six ethical baselines:
   a. Categorical Imperative. This character would have a strong sense of justice. Right is right and wrong is wrong.

    b. Utilitarianism. This character believes in the greatest good for the greatest number of people. The focus is on consequences. He would sacrifice one life to save many.

    c. Hedonism. This is the pleasure principle. This character just wants to have fun. He is selfish.

    d. Golden Mean. This character compromises and negotiates. He will try to find the middle ground to reach a peaceful agreement.

    e. Golden Rule. Do unto others as you would have them do unto you. This character has empathy and compassion.

    f. Veil of Ignorance. This character blissfully goes through life wearing rose-colored glasses. Everything is good, everyone is equal. [1]

2. Is the character dominated by emotion or logic?

3. What is his greatest strength?

4. What is his flaw?
    a. A Hero will be flawed, but the flaw will be redeemable.
    b. A Villain is fatally flawed. Whatever is flawed will be his downfall.

5. How does he see himself?

6. How is he seen by others?

7. What is his biggest secret?

8. What does the character want?

9. How far will the character go to get what he wants?

10. What does the character need to learn?

These questions build what is called a *character profile*. The character profile forms the personality of the character. It is best if these questions are answered with the story and story conflicts in mind. Then you can construct a character that meets the conflicts and drives the story in the way that you intend.

Let's look at a possible profile for Chunk, the main character of *The Animator and the Seat*.

Chunk:

1. Ethical Perspective: Golden Mean.

2. He is dominated by emotion.

3. Greatest Strength: Chunk usually has an unwavering work ethic, incredible talents, and the ability to sound cooler than he really is.

4. Flaw: He is bored with his job.

5. He sees himself as complacent and law abiding.

6. He is seen by others as weak, but a great workhorse. He will go the extra mile to get a project done.

7. Biggest Secret: Has decided he needs a change in employment.

8. What does the character want? A break.

9. How far will the character go to get what he wants? Not very far. He is a pushover. He is extremely excitable when faced with physical threat. He will use all of his will-power to avoid conflict and will give in rather than fight.

10. What does the character need to learn? There are no breaks during crunch time.

Remember in this story that Chunk is an animator who starts to take a break, only to be forced back to work by his chair. His chair has clearly been charged with the task of keeping him in his place—working.

The character profile makes sense when put in relationship to the story and how the character emotionally reacts to the situation in which he finds himself. If your profile doesn't help your character progress through the story, then you need to change your profile or change your story. Don't think of the profile as something that is set in stone. Think of it as a working document that can be refined as you go through the story development process. Characters are constructed. Their personality traits may need adjustment for the good of the story.

Working with Two or More Characters

When working with two or more characters, there is additional information you need to add to the profiles:

1. What is the relationship of your characters?
   Characters have relationships. Did they just meet or do they have a history? Are they strangers, acquaintances, friends, foes, family members, lovers, siblings, enemies? How do they feel toward each other? How does that affect the way they act in the story?

2. What is status of each character?
   Status is defined by how much power you wield in a relationship. The power in a relationship is negotiable. We negotiate status all of the time. In a restaurant the customer is of higher status than the waiter. It is the job of the waiter to serve the customer. But that power shifts if you ask the waiter for a recommendation. Characters will negotiate power by being aggressive, passive, pleasing, assertive, or manipulative. Who has the power in your story and how is it negotiated with the other character(s)?

3. What do they want from each other?
   This is slightly different from the original question, "What does the character want?" In *Gopher Broke*, all of the characters want the same thing. They want vegetables. The gopher wants the other characters to leave the vegetables alone. After all, he has done all the work. The other characters simply don't care. In fact, they are willing to threaten and fight the gopher for the vegetables. This defines the relationship between the gopher and the other characters and becomes the primary conflict.

4. Who is the story about?
   This may seem obvious, but frequently when there are two strong characters, you some-times lose sight of whose story you are telling. Make sure that you keep it clear who the main character really is. Often the main character is the one who arcs the most.

To make a character original, you need to look closely at its character profile. Who is he and what makes him unique as a character? Find this trait and exaggerate it in the design. If your character is a great intellectual, exaggerate the cranium. Give him a big forehead. If your character is a habitual eavesdropper, give her big ears. If a gopher is highly optimistic but slow, give him big eyes, but a heavy lower body. Define what visual attributes are necessary to effectively tell your story.

Sometimes these attributes are defined by what the characters have to *do* in the story. What they have to do give cues to their visual design. In *The Incredibles*, Elastigirl is not just an interesting design for a superhero; she stretches because she is a mother and must always multitask. Dash is fast because he is a little boy with so much pent-up energy. Violet disappears and has a protective shield because she is in adolescence. Elastigirl is organic and loose in the joints. Dash is solid and low to the ground with strong legs. Violet is slim and has hair that perpetually hangs over her large and watchful eyes.

Other ways to find a unique character design is to look at the characters' goals and the conflicts that they must confront. In *The Triplets of Belleville*, Madame Souza's goal is to save her kidnapped grandson, Champion, from the French Mafia. She is small and old. Many obstacles are put in her way: an ocean, lack of money, the city of Belleville, and the Mafia. You would think that this would be enough. But Sylvain Chomet designed her with one leg shorter than the other. She wears one elevated shoe. Because of this, she can move only slowly. There is, in her physical design, an impediment to her goal: to quickly rescue her grandson. It is not enough that she is small and old. We expect grandmothers to be small and old. Her foot makes her different and memorable. The first time we see her we see her foot. It creates intrigue and we want to know more about her.

Similarly, Chris Perry's little girl in *Catch* is made of simple geometric shapes. Her environment is also made up of shapes. The shapes represent the simplicity and innocence of childhood. They contrast sharply with the photographic reality of a grown, well-developed woman in a billboard. The little girl must confront her future and decide what is worthwhile at that time in her life. The design of the character is in direct contrast with the conflict she must face.

Catch, Chris Perry, University of Massachusetts at Amherst

Creating originality and function can be simpler than that. It can be as simple as designing a character who wants to sew on a button but has extremely fat fingers, or a character who needs to scratch an itch but has very short arms.

Finally, there may be times when it is necessary for the design to contrast with the personality traits or functions of the character. In Meng Vue's *The Dancing Thief*, the police woman is defined by her overbearing size and her badge. These are cues that signal how seriously she takes her job and the threat that she poses to the thief. We are surprised and delighted when we discover that she is graceful, loves to dance, and is capable of love.

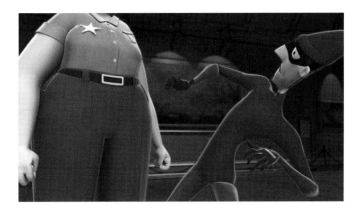

The Dancing Thief, Meng Vue, Ringling College of Art and Design

Remember that the short film needs to deliver more in a smaller time frame. Carefully constructing your character design to immediately convey strong personality traits or character functions will communicate the essence of your character to your audience faster.

Actions, Gestures, and Additional Attributes

The final step to designing your character is to test it against the actions and gestures it will need to perform in the story. If you have designed your character with a big head and short arms, but the story requires him to cross the monkey bars in a playground, you might be in trouble. If you need his mouth to drop to the floor and his tongue to roll out across the room, make sure he is designed in a way that will allow him to do so.

Look at the extremes of the emotional expressions your character needs. The face and the hands are the most expressive parts of the body. How far do they stretch? What kinds of exaggerations are necessary? This becomes a bigger consideration when you begin to model, but at the design stage, you want to make sure that the expressions are readable.

Also think about how detailed the character is and how the design will affect the time it will take to animate it. Things like flowing hair, loose clothing, big bellies, and large feet all

For example, in *Gopher Broke*, we begin the story on a dirt road in the middle of a wheat field. The first thing we see is a sign that points in the direction of the Farmer's Market posted in the rocky dirt on the side of the road. The next thing we see are dandelions. Then we see dandelions in the background disappearing into the earth until the gopher runs into the sign and gets a better idea as a pickup truck loaded with crates and tomatoes (identical to the ones on the sign) drives by. We learn from this introduction that we are in the country. There is a critter who ordinarily eats dandelions but now has an opportunity for something better. The make and model of the truck tell us the time period. Because the story involves several iterations of vegetable displacement from various trucks that drive by, we need to consider the other props we need for the story: trucks—making them the same but different colors will help with feasibility; types of vegetables; types of crates.

Important props, like the sign and the dandelions, need to be prominent. The sign is of particular significance because it is the prop that ultimately causes the demise of the gopher. The gopher, in frustration, throws the sign on the road where it is hit by a truck that careens out of control, catapulting a cow from the back of the truck, which lands on the gopher. The lesson here is that a prop is also never a just a prop. It must be used to convey information or drive the story forward. Be careful not to overpopulate your sets with props. Use only what you need to tell the story. Make sure the props don't steal the scene from the character.

***Gopher Broke* Prop Concept Art by Chuck Wojtkiewicz, Blur Studios**

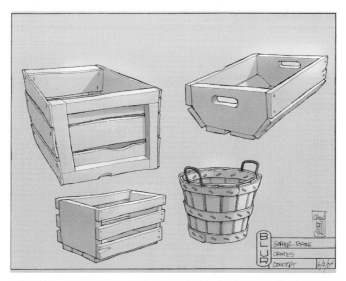

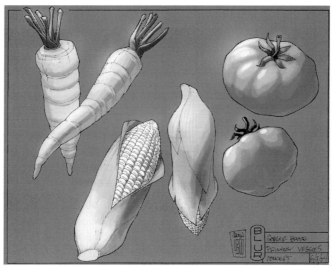

ROUGH +
UNEVEN TIMBERS

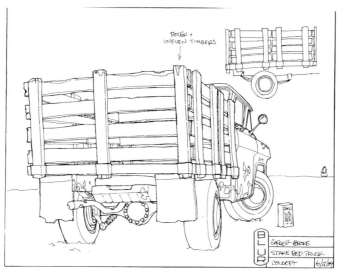

In *The Animator and the Seat*, there is a relatively low level of texture. This supports the boredom of the cubicle and desire of the animator to leave the space. The lack of texture also means there is a lower level of reality present which supports the believability of the unusual occurrences that take place in the space.

Low texture allows for a sense of mystery and the unexpected. *The Animator and the Seat,* Eric Drobile, *Ringling College of Art and Design*

On the other hand, *Respire, Mon Ami* is filled with semi-realistic, heavily textured locations. The reality of these spaces magnifies the weak grasp the boy has on his own sense of what is real.

High texture and detail give a sense of realism. *Respire, Mon Ami,* Chris Nabholtz, **Ringling College of Art and Design**

In *The Kite*, texture is used to support the idea of flight. In an otherwise sparse environment, wisps of grass constantly blow in the wind as a subtle reminder of what the character is trying to achieve: to fly a kite.

Grass in the landscape reinforces the concept of flight. *The Kite*, **Gwynne Wheeler, Ringling College of Art and Design**

- **Color.** Some colors that we use in a scene are dictated by what is called local color. These are colors that have natural associations. Grass is green; the sky is blue; the wood floor is brown, etc. Other colors are used to create emotion through visceral, psychological, or cultural associations. For example, green is associated with nature, growth, and rebirth. But it can also mean lack of experience, good luck, greed, envy, jealousy, or sickness. How can one color generate such a range of possibilities? The range of emotion often has to do with the value or saturation of the color. Yellow-green connotes sickness. Dark green is the color of ambition. Pure green symbolizes healing, safety, and nature. Colors have finite emotional associations. Reds and yellows are warm. Greens and blues are cool. Grays are neutral. Good design requires that you understand the range of emotion that a color can create so you can apply it thoughtfully in your work.
  - Red—warmth, richness, power, excitement, eroticism, romance, anxiety, anger
  - Orange—hot, healthy, exuberant, exhilarated, ambitious, fascinated, exotic, romantic, toxic
  - Yellow—happy, energy, joy, innocence, caution, cowardice
  - Green—vital, successful, healthy, fertile, safe, inexperienced, jealous, ominous, poisonous, corrupt
  - Blue—stable, calm, dependable, tranquil, loyal, sincere, passive, melancholy, cold
  - Purple—wise, dignified, independent, mysterious, mystical
  - White—innocent, good, pure, clean, cold
  - Black—elegant, formal, strong, authoritative, powerful, dangerous, evil, grief, death

For every location in your piece, you will have a color palette that will define the emotion in the scene. The color of the scene may set one mood that remains constant throughout the scene or the color may change with the emotion of the character or the rising intensity of the action to support specific moments in the story.

- **Lighting.** The most important element to creating the mood of your piece is light. Many cinematographers refer to light as the paint for their canvas, the screen. Light is what shows or hides important details, defines shapes, or controls direction. Light sets the atmosphere, the tone, and the drama of the scene through the quality and intensity of the light.

  The quality of light is usually described as hard or soft. A hard light is characterized by a high contrast of bright light, dark shadows, and sharp edges. *Film Noir* is an example of hard light. Hard light creates energy, excitement, suspense, and tension. A soft light is characterized by lower contrast and softer, diffused shadows. Soft lights are often used for more natural settings where the environment requires a more even lighting situation. A soft light is calming. It can also evoke beauty, innocence, tranquility, and romance.

  The intensity of the light refers to the overall brightness of light in a scene and the relative amount of fall-off of the light into shadow. The intensity of light is identified as low key and high key.

  A scene that is low key is dark. It is high in contrast, often lit by a single light source creating deep shadows and patterns of light. The fall-off from light to dark is rapid. Foreground objects are typically seen in silhouette. The most common use of low key lighting is nighttime or stormy weather. However, low key lighting can also create a mood of suspense or alienation. Many horror or thriller films use low key lighting to create the sense of foreboding. Low key lighting can also be used in lower energy scenes that evoke sadness, isolation, or depression.

  High key lighting is bright with light shadows. It is low in contrast. Associated with daylight, high key lighting usually evokes a cheerful, high energy atmosphere but can also support a range of moods. When bright enough it can also be glaring, harsh, or hot.

  Interiors that use high key lighting include corporate offices, grocery stores, hospitals, and institutions. The light in these environments is flat with little fall-off from foreground to background, creating a clean or sterile atmosphere.

  How we choose to light a scene is subjective. Most lighting situations are balanced between light and dark, in the medium gray range, because that is what is considered normal. Altering your lighting situations has dramatic impact on the emotion of your scene. For instance, you might consider using hard lights with low key for a panicked chase scene at night. Or you might use high keys and soft light for that lazy picnic in the country.

  One other factor affecting the energy of the light in your scene is color. All lights have color. Interior lights tend to be yellow while sunlight is white. Fluorescent lights are green. Monitors and television sets emit a blue light. The color of the light will affect the mood of the piece, creating a natural or unnatural setting.

Gopher Broke is piece that uses high key lighting to create the bright afternoon in the country.

Gopher Broke, Jeff Fowler, Blur Studios

Our Special Day begins with a bright yellow palette of light combined with the blue hues of the softer shadows of early morning. The light matches the expectation of the little girl as she waits for her father to arrive. By midday, bored and tired, her hopes diminished, the palette of the piece is orange and brown. The lighting has few shadows and is oppressive. By evening, when the father has not arrived, we have dissolved into reds with low key light, the young girl in silhouette still waiting.

Our Special Day by Fernanda Santiago, Ringling College of Art and Design

The Dancing Thief is set in a museum at night. Most of the piece is lit with spotlights and heavy shadows, creating a dark and theatrical space.

The Dancing Thief, Meng Vue, Ringling College of Art and Design

A Great Big Robot from Outer Space Ate My Homework is also low key with deep shadows to create the tension between the demanding teacher and the young boy in a time before high technology.

A Great Big Robot from Outer Space Ate My Homework, **Mark Shirra, Vancouver Film School**

- **Design Elements.** The line, shape, scale, and directional orientation of the elements in the scene communicate meaning and create style. An environment composed of organic shapes has a very different feeling than one created with geometric shapes. Curves, right angles, and horizontal orientations are calming and stable. Diagonals, pointed edges, repeated verticals, and whacked perspective create energy and tension.

  In *The Animator and the Seat* the perspective and shape of everything in the environment, from the doorway to the bookcase to the desk, is off kilter, creating an environment that is tense like a bad dream. *Catch* uses primary shapes to evoke a sense of childhood. The beginning of the piece is open and round. The forest is large, vertical, and sharp. The scale of the forest creates danger. The billboard scene uses hard verticals to create a feeling that is industrial and cold.

Supporting the Story

Everything about the location—the props, space, texture, color, lighting, and design combine to support the story and communicate the time period, genre, and style of the piece. Styles range from general categories such as realistic, abstract, caricatured, cartooned, exaggerated, organic, and geometric; to specific recognized styles in art such as *Art Deco* or *Film Noir*; to very specific times or locations like Muncie, Indiana, in the 1950s. Don't copy styles from other people. Don't make the style of the piece the way it is because "that is the way you draw." Choose a style that will best enhance your character and tell your story.

Locations are developed in concept art called master sketches or master backgrounds. This is art that is produced to accompany story pitches. It should communicate the atmosphere, lighting, and design of the piece. These pieces should create intrigue, curiosity, and interest in your audience. For the short, you want the visual of your location to get your audience into the story quickly. Just as with your character designs, the location design needs visual interest that makes us want to know more.

The following drawings show two possible variations for a scene that takes place in a grandmother's house. The first is a perfectly acceptable drawing of the living room. It sets the stage, has room for action to take place, and gives a sense of who lives there. It is a passive but functional space.

However, the second drawing has intrigue and implication. It is a location where something has happened and more could happen. It is an active space. The furniture and accessories have been carefully moved to the edges of the room. The rug has been rolled up, the mirror taken off the wall. Tools lie prominently in the foreground and a hole has been broken through the floor. It creates questions in the mind of the audience. Who has done this and why?

Gary Schumer, Ringling College of Art and Design

The first drawing sets the stage, but the second drawing is what you want to sell the piece and to start the story.

Summary

Character:

- A good character is believable, memorable, and right for the story.
- Understanding your character will allow you to create believable reactions to the conflicts in the story.
- Knowing your character comes from creating a back story or character profile.
- The character profile forms the personality of the character.
- When working with two or more characters, you must also establish their relationship, status, and individual goals.
- You must establish which character the story is truly about.
- That character will arc or change, physically, mentally, spiritually, and always emotionally, throughout the course of the story.

A good character design will:

- Be immediately recognizable and relatable.
- Have a recognizable shape.
- Reflect the personality of the character.
- Include physical attributes that complement the content of the story.
- Be able to complete the actions that are required by the script.
- Be interesting to watch.

A good location:

- Sets the stage for the animation through props and space.
- Defines the mood of the piece through texture, color, light, and design.
  - Texture determines the level of reality
  - Color evokes emotion
  - Light creates atmosphere, tone, and drama
  - Design communicates meaning and creates style
- Supports the story.
- A good location design creates intrigue, getting the audience quickly into the story.

Recommended Readings

1. Tom Bancroft, *Creating Characters with Personality For Film, TV, Animation, Video Games and Graphic Novels*

2. Marc McCutcheon, *Building Believable Characters*

3. John Alton, *Painting with Light*

4. Patti Bellantoni, *If It's Purple, Somebody's Gonna Die*

5. *http://www.salon.com/ent/col/srag/1999/08/05/bird/* This is a great interview with Brad Bird that explains how everything in an environment supports the story. If it is still available on line, you should read it.

Notes

[1] Ollie Johnston and Frank Thomas, *The Illusion of Life*, Disney Editions, Revised sub-Edition, 1995, p. 68.

[2] Lester, Paul, *Visual Communication: Images with Messages*, 4th edition, Wadsworth Publishing, 2005.

The names of the six ethical perspectives come from Paul Lester's book. The definitions have been modified for simplicity and space. For deeper definitions of these terms, please refer to Paul Lester's book.

[3] Quotes from the *Making of Belleville*, by permission of Sylvain Chomet.

Personality, Goals, Shapes, and Variance in Character Design: Tom Bancroft, Funnypages Productions, LLC

Tom Bancroft is a partner in Funnypages Productions, LLC, a company that provides illustration, character design, and artistic animation development for clients such as Disney, DC comics, Big Idea Productions, Warner Brothers, CBN, Scholastic, NavPress, Thomas Nelson, and Zondervan. FP Productions has also developed many original properties for film and television and illustrated over 30 children's books. Prior to Funnypages, Tom worked for Walt Disney Feature Animation (WDFA) on both shorts and features films including *Beauty and the Beast*, *The Lion King*, *Aladdin*, *Mulan*, *Lilo and Stitch*, and *Brother Bear*. Tom is the author of *Creating Characters with Personality*, published by Watson-Guptill Publishers.

Tom: For this book, I was asked to contribute some of my thoughts on the subject of character design. I've known Gary Schumer for years and he thought of me because of my book on the subject, *Creating Characters with Personality*. Just because I wrote and illustrated a book on the subject, I never feel that I "know it all." I believe that as an artist, as in life, the moment you stop learning is the moment you start dying.

I don't have much room here to go into all the nuances of character design, but I did want to hit four main principles that you should think about when designing a character:

Personality

You don't want a bland, generic character, right? So, don't just think: "I want to draw a cute, little bear." Think: "I want to design a bear that is kind of lazy and only motivated to go fishing (his one true love). He knows everything about fishing, but won't do anything around the house for his wife. In high school he was a football champ, but has since let himself go because he doesn't need much strength for fishing. He is a likeable guy though." Now you're ready to design a character with a personality. Knowing what you are designing is job one.

Goals

It's important to know what, why, and how you want to design this character. Make some goals. If this character is not just for fun but for a client, then you will have a lot of the "goals" of what you need to design given to you. Is it for a certain age group? Do you want it to be cute or just appealing (there is a difference)? Does it have to do anything special, such as run fast, look pretty/sexy, look a certain age, etc.? Is there a style that you are trying to accomplish? Should it look realistic or extremely cartoony? All these things should be thought about or discussed before pencil hits paper. After all, without goals, how do you know when you are done?

Shapes

When I start drawing, the first things I start thinking of are what shapes will make up this character. If it's a happy, thick character, I will start working with circle shapes. A strong, firm kind of character would get squares. A thin, wimpy kind of character might be rectangles or ovals. You always want to be able to break your character down into basic shapes so that you (or others) can duplicate that character in a variety of different angles, poses, or expressions.

Variance

The next page shows some designs that I created for a made-up assignment. First, let me state my goals:

> I am trying to design an extremely cute girl character, around 6–8 years old, who has a "devilish" side to her. Style-wise, I'm going for a pretty cartoony style too. It's for TV, so it needs to be a fairly simplified design also.

As you can see by the designs (and they are numbered in the order I produced them), that I didn't decide I "had it" after the first design. I kept refining and trying different shapes and sizes of things. One will have longer legs and a short torso. The next will have a big head, medium torso, and short legs. One has small eyes that are close together; another, large eyes that are farther apart. In short, I am adding "variance" to the designs. That's variance—using shape and size in various ways to create different designs. Which one would I pick as my favorite? I'll let you decide which one met the above goals the best. Enjoy the challenges of creating characters with personality!

Chapter 5

Building Story

In this chapter, we will discuss strategies for building the animated short story.

To build a short, you need the following:

- A theme or concept
- A character(s)
- A location
- A situation
- A rising conflict
- An ending

In previous chapters we covered the concepts of theme, character(s), location, situation, and conflict. By now, you should have a basic working premise for your idea. A premise is one or two sentences describing your character, situation and, conflict. It is the basic setup for what happens in the story.

This chapter focuses on developing the premise into a story, learning story structure, building a rising conflict, and understanding the function of endings.

Solving Problems

Every story is unique and has its own individual problems. Using the strategies we discuss in this chapter, you will be able to identify the problems in your story and fix them.

The most common pitfall in story development is that rather than identifying and solving problems that need to be solved the storyteller either adds more—more characters, more conflicts, more props, more stuff—or continually changes the core of the story, reinventing it as a brand new story. This brings them back to square one, to the beginning of the process. Every time you start a new story, even a variation on a theme, you will have new set of problems that need to be solved.

As you solve problems, your story will change. This change means everything to a successful product. We tend to be completion-oriented. But story development, by its definition, requires process: the generation of options, the exploration of possibilities, and the ruthlessness to be able to take out the trash or cut the things you love for the good of the piece. Working through it again and again is part of the process.

All stories begin with anticipation and passion that at some point meet with hesitation or frustration before breaking through to find the inspiration that makes the story work. Know that it is worth the work. Pursue your story.

So You Think You Have a Story Idea: Developing the Premise

Once you have a basic premise, the tendency is to rush forward and immediately begin to develop conflict and plot points. Before you do this, pause and make sure your premise is the *best* execution for your idea. What does that mean? When working on a short, you have one idea to communicate. You want to find the most entertaining way to reach your audience. You also want to make sure it is feasible to produce. Finally, you unequivocally **need** to be able to say that animation is the best medium for this piece.

A good short idea has one or two characters, limited locations, and ONE conflict that becomes worse. If you have multiple characters, multiple locations, or multiple conflicts, take time now, not later, to simplify, clarify, and revise.

Example:

Premise: On the school playground, Sarah Jenkins, a developing adolescent, is taunted by her slightly younger friends as she hits puberty.

Theme or concept: Some of us grow faster than others, but it is going to happen to everyone.

The premise has some problems:

- It has multiple human characters—Sarah and her peer(s). Humans are still hard to animate well.
- The location, a playground, has multiple items to model.
- The conflict—taunting—while singular is not yet very visual and seems to require the use of dialogue.
- Sarah's development would probably include hips, breasts, pimples, and greasy hair. How do you make the physicality of adolescence appealing?

All of this has the making of a live-action after school special, but it's too complex, and lacks a compelling reason to animate. Since this is the premise you want to develop, and you're passionate about it, the question becomes how do we improve it?

Stories have essentials that must be kept. In this story, the essentials include Sarah, development, taunting, and Sarah's desire to belong. Everything else can be swapped out. It is easy enough to change the peers to a single friend or better yet to a sibling. Likewise, the location can be moved from the school playground to almost anywhere else—maybe the dressing room in a department store. Unfortunately, this is still better for live action than animation. The set-up lacks appeal.

Don't abandon the idea yet. Instead, start to generate options. Look at character, genre, time period, place, and point of view. Any of these might spark a new set-up that is more entertaining.

Character

What do we already know about Sarah? She is an adolescent girl. She develops. Could Sarah be something else that develops in a more interesting and visual way? What if she is an egg that hatches? What if she is a caterpillar that cocoons into a butterfly? What if she is an insect or a toy machine—a transformer? Write "what if's" until you find lots of creative options . . . maybe a tadpole.

Genre

Sometimes situation and conflict gain more interest when played through a different genre. What happens to this story if, instead of an after school special, it becomes a sci-fi film? Other genres include:

- Documentary
- Action adventure
- Coming of age
- Horror
- Comedy
- Sports
- Western
- Musical
- War
- Fantasy

Playing your idea through each genre should give you additional ideas. Sports: What if Sarah has always been a competitive athlete and is so good that she qualifies for boys' teams. What implication does her development have on her ability to compete?

Time and Place

Many beginning short ideas start out in a contemporary time period and setting with characters that are very much like the author. This is because stories are about us—and we have been repeatedly told to write (or draw) what we know. However, a change in time or place sometimes raises the appeal of the story. What if Sarah is competing on U.S. boys' teams in the early 1950s? What if she is competing in ancient Greece?

What if the story takes place during prehistoric time and Sarah becomes Noggin, taunted by Bellyfaces because she has a head?

***Noggin*, directed by Alex Cannon, Brigham Young University**

Point of View

Whose story is it? Right now, it is Sarah's. Would it be a better story, or would we learn a better lesson, if it was told through the eyes of the friend? What if the story was told from the viewpoint of a teacher, mother, the playground, or the body parts? What do you think will resonate most with an audience?

Early Bloomer

Sony Pictures Imageworks told this story through the eyes of a tadpole that begins its transformation just ahead of its peers. It works well because:

- It displaces a common and overused theme to something fresh and new.
- It is told from the *point of view* of a tadpole.
- It takes us to a new *place*, underwater, where we are not sure exactly what we will find.
- Tadpole metamorphosis follows a visual pattern over a relatively short amount of time. The feet and arms can "pop" from the body adding surprise and entertainment.

- All tadpoles look the same to us so, aside from color, all the models are the same. There is still a lot to animate but suddenly we are in the realm of feasibility for the individual animator.

- Underwater is a hard place to be for an animator, but thinking carefully about style choices often makes this feasible as well.

- It allows us to look at a time that was awkward for many of us with empathy and humor.

- It turns teenage angst into a *comedy*.

- It maintains the essentials of the premise while adding appeal and entertainment value.

- It works as an animation because the characters are stylized and the medium provides imaginative possibilities.

New Premise: A green tadpole is taunted by her slightly smaller friends as she begins her transformation into a frog.

Theme or concept: Some of us grow faster than others, but it is going to happen to everyone.

Story Structure

Just as the Hero's Journey provides the basic structure for most feature films, there is a basic structure for linear short animations:

- **Exposition**: The main character and location are introduced. The character may or may not be flawed, but we immediately know who he or she is and what he or she **wants**.

    Early Bloomer: One young, slightly larger green tadpole struggles to keep up with her four slightly smaller playmates in a game of follow the leader.

- **Inciting Incident**: Something unexpected happens that throws the character into action and in pursuit of a **goal**.

   They all swim through a broken soda bottle and, bringing up the rear, the slightly larger green one gets stuck in the neck, barely able to squeeze herself through. When she does, her friends are far ahead.

- **Rising conflict**: Something or someone gets in the way of the character reaching the goal. This one conflict gets **worse**. This is usually shown using two to three events.

   Conflict 1: *As she struggles to catch up, her friends swim back to her only to stop short in shock: She's got LEGS!*

Conflict 2: *She tries without success to make her legs stay behind her like a tail.*

Conflict 3: *She is terribly hurt and swims away when her friends make fun of her using plants or each other as legs, and gleefully dance the cancan.*

- **Crisis**: This is the point when the character is at his lowest and the obstacle or conflict is at its highest. The character makes a decision, figures out a problem, finds a magic object, **learns** a lesson, etc.

  As the tadpole sits alone and dejected, her friends approach smiling. She recoils and prepares to defend herself.

- **Climax**: Puts the character in direct conflict with the obstacle. This is the point of no return. The character must **act**. Often in the short, the crisis and the climax become one event.

  At that moment, they show her that they have legs too and she must choose if she will be their friend again or not.

- **Resolution**: The character succeeds or fails.

    Gleefully she shivers with joy when—pop!—open arms of acceptance burst from her body . . . and the smiles on her friends' faces fade as they get a clear picture of what is ahead for them too.

***Early Bloomer,* Director Sande Scoredos, Sony Pictures Imageworks**

At each point in the structure using just a few sentences, unencumbered with details, you can see if your story is working at its fundamental level early on. Is the character's goal clear? Is there an inciting incident? Does the conflict rise? How many conflicts do you have? What does the character learn? How does it end? Does your ending answer the questions raised in the story?

Variations on Linear Structure

There are variations on the basic linear structure outlined above. The main variations that work for the short include:

1. Parallel Structure

With parallel structure, more than one event is going on at the same time during the story. Usually these events eventually converge. For example, in *Ritterschlag*, an adult dragon trains his young offspring to slay knights to keep a princess captive. Believing training is over for the day when the adult dragon falls asleep, the young dragon keeps on practicing. When the young dragon loses the princess, the adult dragon wakes up and rejoins the story.

***Ritterschlag,* directed by Sven Martin, Filmakademie Baden-Wurttemberg, Germany**

2. Circular Structure

In circular structure, the character or story ends up more or less where it began.

Eureka is an example of a circular structure. In this animation, a genius professor goes to work and generates ideas, visualized by a light bulb above his head. One day, his light bulb goes out and he has no ideas. In a series of frustrated attempts to re-light his bulb, he mistakenly reconfigures the way the light bulb works. The character begins with getting ideas visualized by the glowing light bulb and ends getting even better ideas, visualized by a glowing light bulb.

Beginning   **End**
Eureka!, **Parrish Ley, Sheridan College**

Other examples include *The Animator and the Seat.* The animator starts out tired and needing a break and ends up still tired, still needing a break, but with no hope of getting one.

In *Our Special Day,* a little girl begins her day waiting for her father to arrive to take her out and ends up at night, still waiting and still hopeful.

Stan Howard, animation writer, points out that this structure is commonly used for serial cartoons where, at the end of the day, the hero must be restored to himself to start another adventure tomorrow. Jimmy Neutron, SpongeBob SquarePants, Scooby Doo, and Teen Titans go through a series of adventures in every episode. These characters may arc within the episode itself, but by the end, they are essentially unchanged. [1]

3. Bus-Stop Structure

Stan Howard, describes this structure as one where an essential secondary character arrives and leaves during various parts in a story. "It is a bit like people getting on and off a bus." The example he gives is Cinderella's godmother, who arrives, solves a problem, and then leaves. [2]

In *Das Floss*, the seagull plays this role. Two men have been adrift on a raft at sea for many days. They watch as a seagull catches a fish and lands on their mast to eat it. The seagull drops the fish onto the raft, causing conflict for food between two hungry men, and then flies away.

Das Floss, directed by Jan Thuring, Filmakademie Baden-Wurttemberg, Germany

Often these characters arrive to solve a problem, create a problem, or deliver a message. They are small roles, but without them, the story cannot progress.

4. Ping-Pong or Zig-Zag Structure

In this structure, the character moves back and forth between similar but escalating obstacles and similar attempts at resolution. Often the obstacles are new characters that arrive as the old ones leave.

In *Gopher Broke,* a gopher digs holes in a road causing a Produce Truck to bounce, making vegetables fall from the truck. Each time the gopher successfully gets vegetables on the ground, some other creature steals them before he can get to them: first a squirrel, and then a mean chicken, and finally a flock of crows. Each event sends him back to try again. He ping-pongs between the same attempt to get vegetables and similar but escalating defeats. (See image on opposite page.)

The *ChubbChubbs*: A Case Study in Structure

The *ChubbChubbs* is a complex short that uses several of these structures in the production of the piece. It is interesting to look at how the different structures drive the plot forward.

In the *ChubbChubbs*, Meeper, a lowly janitor/busboy, is cleaning up at the Ale-E-Inn Pub in outer space. Meeper dreams of being a karaoke singer like the diva in the bar. As she

Gopher Broke, directed by Jeff Fowler, Blur Studios

sings *Respect*, Meeper accidentally knocks over his bucket of water, electrocuting both the microphone and the diva. He is promptly kicked out of the bar, mop and bucket following. As he sits there, Jar Jar Banks climbs over the edge of the world and announces that the ChubbChubbs are coming and then promptly passes out.

Meeper, wondering who the ChubbChubbs might be, looks and sees a huge dust cloud from an approaching alien army. Assuming these are the ChubbChubbs, he runs into the bar to warn the patrons. He slams open the door but before he can utter a word, the patrons gasp. He has smashed the karaoke diva behind the door. He is immediately thrown out of the bar again. This time the door is locked behind him.

The dust cloud is getting closer. He climbs up on the roof to warn the patrons, falls through, and lands on top of the diva. Just as he is bemoaning that he's not very good at this, the door to the pub opens and another character announces that the ChubbChubbs are coming. Everyone panics and flees.

Meeper, trying to keep people calm, sees the dust cloud again and thinks that maybe it really is a good time to panic. At the same time, he spies some innocent chicks pecking at the ground unaware of the impending danger. Just as he manages to scoop up the chicks in his bucket, the army arrives. Meeper asks if they can be friends and breaks into a karaoke routine, singing, *"Why Can't We Be Friends?"* The army responds by threatening Meeper.

At this point, the chicks emerge from the bucket and attack the army, defending Meeper. They are the ChubbChubbs. They happily trot back to Meeper. He hesitantly accepts their friendship. With their support he secures a place as a karaoke singer where the patrons, under threat of the ChubbChubbs, cheer him.

Parallel Structure: While the alien army approaches the rest of the story progresses. There are cuts between the impending army and Meeper's attempts to get back to the bar.

Bus-Stop Structure: Both Jar Jar Banks and the unknown alien that finally announce the impending arrival of the ChubbChubbs are heralds that drop into the story, announce important pieces of information, and then disappear.

Zig-Zag or Ping-Pong: Meeper hurts the object of his desire, the karaoke diva (unwittingly eliminating the competition for his dream job), and is thrown out of the pub. He goes back to the pub and again smashes the diva. He is thrown back out. He goes back in and lands on the diva from above. He is forced back out by the panicking patrons.

Circular Structure: This is very minor. But the patrons of the pub end up nearly where they began. In the beginning, they are applauding the karaoke diva. In the end, they are hesitantly applauding the poor crooning of Meeper. This helps bring a sense of closure to the piece.

***The ChubbChubbs,* directed by Eric Armstrong, Sony Pictures Imageworks**

ENDINGS: The Importance of Knowing Where You Are Going

So by now you know how to improve a premise. You understand the elements of linear structure and where they fit in a story. You understand variations so that you can determine how your story might progress. The next step would be to write the progression of the conflicts, right?

Not yet. Before you write the progression of conflicts, you need to know where you are headed.

Ending stories well is harder than you might think. Often the story moves along smoothly and ends, but the conclusion is flat. Creating a good ending is a challenge. It takes the tenacity to think through all the ways it could happen, searching for the one that transforms your character, your audience, or both.

Let's say that again. You are searching for an ending that transforms the character, the audience, or both.

Endings Are Like Cheesecake

Tonight, you are going to an expensive restaurant. There is background music, white table-cloths, atmosphere, and those waiters that carry towels on their forearms and meet your every need. You never do this. It is a special occasion.

The company and conversation are perfect. Everything from the drinks to the appetizers to all seven courses is superb. It is time for dessert. You never get dessert. But, tonight, everything has been so special that you will. You order cheesecake. It's your favorite.

When the cheesecake arrives, it is a very small piece slightly tilting on a white plate. The waiter leaves his fingerprints on the side of the plate. The plate is greasy. You notice a tiny piece of cardboard stuck to the graham cracker crust. The restaurant buys its cheesecake. It's packaged.

What did this just do to your evening?

Now imagine the cheesecake arriving . . . it is an ample creamy slice resting on a beautiful hand-blown cobalt blue plate. At its edge are three perfectly sliced pieces of green kiwi. Raspberry sauce is drizzled back and forth across the cake in gently curving ripples. You take a bite. It is so light it barely glazes your tongue and you nearly float to the ceiling.

How is your evening now? Are you going back to the restaurant?

Endings and Beginnings

James Mercurio, screenwriter, teacher and lecturer, believes you must know your ending first to really understand and write your beginning and determine the proper progression of conflict. In order to know your ending you must understand what your piece means—the theme, concept, or idea communicated by the animation. [5]

This is because the theme or meaning of the piece directs the resolution. The theme is revealed in story structure in the climax of the story. Whatever your character learns usually communicates the theme of the piece. The decision he makes, how he chooses to act against his opposition, determines the ending.

When Shrek sits broken hearted in the swamp, Donkey convinces him to tell Fiona he loves her. Shrek realizes that he both wants and deserves love (realization of the theme). He goes to try to defeat Farquaad and win his girl (the act that determines the ending).

In *Early Bloomer,* when the tadpole is confronted by her friends, she learns that eventually everyone develops. Then she chooses to forgive her friends.

When the ChubbChubbs scramble back to Meeper after defeating the alien army, Meeper learns that he has the power to get some respect. Meeper chooses to use this power to achieve his dream.

In the resolution or ending, the character succeeds or fails and must do so in a way that he or the audience arcs emotionally. Hopefully the ending does this in a way that is unpredictable.

In Shrek, when Fiona finds true love she is suppose to take true love's "form." Both Fiona and the audience expect that she will assume the beautiful form of a princess. Instead, she turns into an ogre. And she is fine with it because this is the form of her true love, Shrek. We expect Shrek and Fiona to end up together, but this ending does it in a way that is both perfectly aligned with the story and is also unpredictable.

The tadpole accepts her friends back only to progress to the next stage of development. Pop. Now there are arms and hands! Oh no! Surprise!

The storytellers hold back on what the new friendship between Meeper and the Chubb-Chubbs means until, after the credits, when we see Meeper singing badly, fulfilling his dream in front of a hesitant audience.

Once we know the ending, we can reveal something more about the character in the beginning.

In the beginning of the *ChubbChubbs*, Meeper is portrayed as the lowest character in the bar, the janitor. As he moves through the bar, we hear him speak to customers and learn that he is caring, helpful, and dedicated to his job. He daydreams that he is the respected karaoke singer on stage. At one point, an Aretha Franklin-esque character is on stage singing the song *Respect*, the theme of the piece.

As he daydreams, he uses his broom as a microphone and subsequently knocks over his bucket of water, frying both the microphone and electrocuting the object of his desire, the singer—unconsciously eliminating the competition. Meeper is kicked out of the bar and shows that he is tenacious, "I'll just take this as my break."

You cannot write this opening or choose this song if you don't know that at the end Meeper gains a position as a karaoke singer and, with the help of the ChubbChubbs, at least feigned respect from the audience.

In the beginning of *Early Bloomer*, the tadpole struggles determinedly with her equilibrium. You can't show this if you don't know that in the end she is going to continue to develop, shock her friends, and need to win their acceptance.

In the opening scene of Shrek, he uses a fairytale princess book as toilet paper. In fact, he uses the very princess he is destined to fall in love with and he does it with great disbelief and disdain. You can't write this opening if you don't know your ending.

Finding Your Ending

There are two ways to find an ending: Straight Ahead and Strategic Planning.

1. Straight Ahead

In this method, you start with what you know: your premise. You begin your piece, building your plot points by asking, "What happens next?" The question continues until you find a way for the story to end. Even when you think you have found your ending, you continue the questioning for a few more beats. Sometimes the best answer is still a little bit further down the road.

This is an intuitive method. It is useful because you usually build many plot points along the way and it is easy to try it over and over. It is difficult because it can build a very large story that must be edited down considerably. There is great possibility for the story to wander, lose focus, or go off track. When it feels like this is happening, you will need to determine if you have a false start or if you have a story that really doesn't work.

If you use this method, have someone record the session, either with notes or video, because as you are talking or acting your way through the story, you will forget some of the wonderful ideas that emerged in the process.

2. Strategic Planning

It usually involves concentrating on the relationship between the exposition, the meaning of the piece and how it resolves. It takes as much experimentation and brainstorming as working straight ahead, but the focus is on generating multiple possibilities of how the ending occurs, conceptually, visually, and emotionally. Draw it out. Remember that your piece is visual. Sometimes it is the visual that sells the ending. In *Early Bloomer,* the expressions and gestures of all of the characters at the end would be difficult to sell with words. The images are immediate.

Happy Endings

Let's go back to *Early Bloomer* and look at the ending. *Early Bloomer,* like many animated shorts, does not exactly have a happy ending. It is a funny ending, but not a happy one. The character's goal is to be like her friends. When her friends realize, to their dismay, that they are going to be like her—none of them is sure what that means.

In feature films a happy ending is often a requirement. In the animated short, it is easier to end with a spiral downward, a failure, or sad ending. The reason is both administrative and budgetary. When making a short, frequently you have no one to answer to but yourself. There are no outside directors and producers who have a stake in the content and the box-office success of your piece. In the short, making money is often not the priority. Therefore, you are free to tell the story you want to tell the way you want to tell it.

Additionally, because in the short you must get in quick—the inciting incident should happen in the first 15 to 20 seconds of your film—and get out quick, the audience is more emotionally accepting of a piece where the character fails, particularly if that failure is ironic, satiric, or in some way makes us think or laugh.

In *Early Bloomer,* the audience is located in a different emotional place from the characters. The characters have angst. The majority of the audience, having gone through puberty, is both amused and grateful they never have to do that again. Those in puberty or pre-puberty may identify more with the characters and find a way to laugh at themselves. How do you want your audience to feel after they watch *your* piece?

Building Conflict

Now that you know how your story begins and ends, the challenge is to build conflict in a way that engages the audience. Remember in the short that there is no time to deviate from the focus of the story, the goal of the character, or the single problem the character must overcome.

When building conflict it is helpful to think about the way the conflict unfolds, the type of intensity building, the character in the conflict, and the location of your audience in your story.

Progression of Conflict

Often when beginning storytellers think of conflict, they default to the catastrophic. They think about *big* problems. Problems don't have to be big to cause conflict. An itch, a headache, or a stubbed toe can all have great affect and be wonderful inspiration for story. But if you scratch an itch, take medicine, or put ice on your toe, the story is over. These are single events that cause a problem and can be easily resolved. To build story conflict, the conflict has to get worse. Scratching an itch leads to itching all over that leads to a spreading rash that lands you in the hospital where you meet a pretty nurse that catches your rash . . . .

In story, the progression of the conflict for the character occurs in predictable ways:

1. **Compounded Conflicts**: A **single** problem builds in layers upon itself through **similar** or **related** events. Compounded problems follow two patterns:
   - Domino Effect. This is a chain reaction where one problem will cause a similar problem to occur in a linear sequence. In *Early Bloomer*, the tadpole has grown slightly bigger only to gain legs and then arms with more to come. The physical problem of growing more body parts layers upon itself to make the situation worse.
   - Cascade Effect #1. One problem will cause a similar problem to occur in a branching structure. A large snowball is rolling down a hill toward a ski lodge. The snowball hits a tree and breaks into two large snowballs rolling down toward the ski lodge. Both of these snowballs hit trees and break in to four, and so on, until an avalanche of snowballs threatens the lodge.

2. **Accumulated Conflicts**: **Multiple** problems build in number or complexity through **different** or **unrelated** events. Accumulated problems follow three patterns:
   - Cascade Effect #2: A change in one event will lead to a change in multiple subsequent events. This is the philosophy behind cascading formats in web design. If you change a logo on one page, it will automatically change in all other places that the logo appears. In story, this is often used with concepts of the time and timelines. If we change events in the past, we can affect the multiple events of the future in unpredictable ways.
   - Ripple Effect. One event leads to other unrelated events that spread out, escalating in all directions. Gobelins, an animation school in France, produced a short called *Le*

Building. In this short, a man is singing in his shower. Next door, an old woman pounds on the wall to get him to stop. The pounding causes her cat to fall out a window into laundry hanging out to dry. The cat trampolines off the laundry into the face of a pizza delivery boy on a scooter. The scooter nearly collides with a bus. The bus crashes into the base of a crane. Missing the bus, the boy on the scooter rides up the stairs of the apartment building where his pizza flies through the mail slot of an apartment onto the bathroom floor just as a woman is stepping out of the tub. She slips on the pizza, grabbing a shelf to catch her fall. The shelf breaks, sending a boom box into the face of the crane operator. The crane operator passes out and hits the lever sending a giant magnet spinning in circles. The magnet picks up the bus and sends it into the building, knocking out the guy who was singing in the shower. The old woman settles down in her chair unaware that the building is barely standing while a bus full of screaming passengers continues in circles.

Ripple effects require a number of events because problems spread out in all directions. It is often difficult, in a short, to have events spread out and be able to bring them back to resolution. *Le Building* was a traditional animation and a group project. It would be difficult to execute this in 3D as an individual or small group.

- The Butterfly Effect. This is the age-old theory that if a butterfly flaps its wings in Australia it will create tiny changes in the atmosphere that have nonlinear and catastrophic effects (hurricane, tidal wave) elsewhere in the world. [5]

Increasing the Intensity of the Conflict

In the short, most conflicts are compounded. All conflicts must rise in intensity until the character is in crisis. Again, crisis doesn't have to mean chaos or catastrophic devastation. It means the character reached the lowest point in the story where he or she learns a lesson, makes a decision, figures out the problem, and so on. It can be small. It can be just an itch.

One of the common problems in story development is that multiple events are created for the character to overcome, but the events do not rise in intensity. The story doesn't really go anywhere.

Increasing intensity has to do with raising the magnitude of a problem in a specific way. Some of the ways are to raise the magnitude of the:

- Physical Obstacle
- Physical Jeopardy
- Mental Jeopardy
- Activity
- Energy
- Strength
- Competition

- Completion
- Volume

These compound as the need for the character to resolve the conflict becomes greater.

The Character in Conflict

The story is the character's story. The plot is driven not by the action presented or required by the conflict, but by the reaction of the character to the problem. Depending on who your character is, what her strengths and weaknesses are, her history, moral position, and whether she operates primarily from a position of logic or emotion will cause the character to respond toward a problem in one of four ways:

- Physically
- Emotionally
- Strategically
- Critically

The character may react in just one way or in all of these ways as she explores different tactics to resolve the conflict. These tactics include:

- Avoiding
- Preventing
- Controlling
- Negotiating
- Attacking

These tactics are driven by the character's thoughts and emotions. Thought and emotion drive her action and reaction. Emotion is evoked in the character because there is something at stake for the character. What is at stake for the character usually has to do with loss of status or power:

- Control
- Acceptance
- Reputation
- Freedom
- Self-esteem
- Health

Emotional changes in the character occur as each event in the story puts what is at stake in jeopardy. These emotional changes are called a *character arc*. Every character, at every point in the story, is thinking and feeling something. This is called *internal monologue*. When you understand what the character is thinking and feeling, you can determine the most truthful way for the character to react to the conflict. You can also alter the internal monologue by trying different tactics to find which are most entertaining to your audience.

If you are having trouble writing conflict events, it is helpful to write out, or talk out what the character is thinking. This helps clarify where the story needs to go or identifies when the character or conflict has deviated from the focus of the story.

If you know what your character is thinking or feeling, you also know what he is doing—and the intensity of emotion with which he is doing it. This gives you the weight and force of the action. When you know what he is doing and how he is doing it—you can draw strong poses in your storyboards.

Putting It Together

The last thing we need to do is understand how conflict relates to the beginning and ending of the story. To do this we are going to look at our basic story structure again. The last time we looked at this we analyzed what happened in each stage of the story. Now we are going to look at how these elements relate to each other.

Exposition: The character will say or do something that reveals a character trait that establishes his outlook on life.

Inciting Moment: Something unexpected happens and the reaction of the character establishes how he will react to future rising conflicts: physically, emotionally, critically, or strategically.

Rising Conflict: As obstacles increase, the character will attempt different tactics to overcome or resolve the conflict. How the character acts and reacts depends on the connection established in the exposition and inciting moment.

Contrast is the key to conflict. If you have a good character, put her against a bad character. If the character needs to reach something high on a shelf, make the character short. Contrast can also be used for how she makes decisions or uses tactics. Make one approach the conflict physically and the other approach emotionally. Make them use opposing tactics. Have one use negotiation and the other use control.

Remember that emotion drives the story. As the conflict escalates in intensity, the emotional state of the character will escalate or deflate exponentially.

Crisis/Climax: It is in the crisis/climax that the character can change how he approaches the problem. If the character has acted emotionally, he may now act physically as an arc occurs in the character.

The character learns something, overcomes his flaw, lets go of what is holding him back, discovers the solution to the problem, and confronts the obstacle. What the character learns makes clear the theme of your piece.

Ending/Resolution: In the end, the character is transformed. The character attributes established in the exposition will have caused the character to succeed or fail. The character is lower or higher, but not the same as when he was introduced.

By using a simple table, you can track how the elements are operating in your story. *Early Bloomer* is used as a case study for the table below.

Title: *Early Bloomer*

Theme or Concept: Some of us grow faster than others, but it is going to happen to us all.

New Premise: A green tadpole is taunted by her slightly smaller friends as she begins her transformation into a frog.

Genre: Coming of Age

Time: Sometime after the invention of glass

Place: Underwater

Point of View: The Green Tadpole

Story Structure: Linear

Story	Emotion	Character Response	Tactic Attempted	What Is at Stake	Intensity of Conflict Raised	Audience Location
Exposition: A young, slightly larger green tadpole struggles to keep up with her slightly smaller playmates in a game of follow the leader. She is having trouble with her equilibrium.	Desire Determination					With the Character
Character Reaction: Green tadpole sticks out her tongue, gathering muster and determined to follow.						

Story	Emotion	Character Response	Tactic Attempted	What Is at Stake	Intensity of Conflict Raised	Audience Location
Inciting Moment: They all swim through a broken soda bottle and, bringing up the rear, the little green one gets stuck in the neck, barely able to squeeze herself through. When she does, her friends are far ahead.					Physical	With the Character
Character Reaction: Green tadpole: She is surprised that she didn't fit through like her friends. She twists and squeezes until she pops out of the bottle. She smiles as her friends swim toward her.	Dismay Disbelief	Physically	Control			
Conflict 1: As she struggles to catch up, her friends swim back to her only to stop short, piling into each other and staring. She's got legs!					Mental	With the Character
Character Reaction: Group: They are in shock. Then they whisper among themselves and stare. Green tadpole: She smiles uncertainly as she follows their gaze and realizes, "She's got legs!"	Group: Astonishment Tadpole: Shock	Emotionally		Acceptance		
Conflict 2: She tries without success to make the legs stay behind her like a tail. There are 3 attempts. She swims hard hoping the currents will keep her legs behind her, but they drift downward when she stops. She spins in circles, but the legs drift down.			Control		Physical + Energy	With the Character

Story	Emotion	Character Response	Tactic Attempted	What Is at Stake	Intensity of Conflict Raised	Audience Location
Character Reaction: Green tadpole: Each time she finds her legs won't stay behind her, she tries something new.	Panic Shame	Physically		Control		
Conflict 3: She swims towards her friends who swim away from her.					Mental	With the Character
Character Reaction: Group: The group makes fun of her using plants as legs, each other as legs, and gleefully dancing the cancan. Green tadpole: At first she is curious about what they are doing, then she swims away dejected as she realizes they are making fun of her.	Group: Amusement Tadpole: Shame Hurt	Emotionally	Group: Attack Tadpole: Negotiate	Self-esteem		
Exposition: After the green tadpole leaves, one by one the others get their legs.						Ahead of the Character
Character Reaction: Group: Each is surprised as legs pop out from the others. They look from one to another and back again.	Surprise Confusion	Emotionally				
Crisis Moment: As the tadpole sits alone and dejected, her friends approach smiling.					Physical	Ahead of the Character
Character Reaction: Green tadpole: She recoils and prepares to defend herself.	Defensive Angry	Critically	Prevent	Acceptance		

Story	Emotion	Character Response	Tactic Attempted	What Is at Stake	Intensity of Conflict Raised	Audience Location
Climax: At that moment, they show her that they have legs too and she must choose if she will be their friend again or not.						With the Character
Character Reactions: She brightens at the sight of their legs and her face breaks into a huge smile.	Happy	Physically	Negotiate			
Resolution: Gleefully she shivers with joy when—pop!—open arms of acceptance burst from her body . . . and the smiles on her friends' faces fade as they get a clear picture of what is ahead for them too.						With the Character
Character Reaction: Green tadpole: Oh-oh. Group: Oh-oh.	Astonishment Apprehension	Emotionally		Acceptance		

The Audience in Story

The role of the storyteller is to take your audience on a journey and to make them feel something at the end. As the storyteller, you control not only where your audience goes, but how they get there. The audience watches your story from four different points of view:

- The audience is located behind the character in the story. The audience knows less than the character. This creates mystery, surprise, or humor.
- The audience learns as the character learns. This creates suspense.
- The audience knows more than the character. This creates tension and drama.
- The audience *thinks* it knows more than the character but the resolution is something different. This creates irony.

The audience is thinking and feeling something at every point in your story. This is called the *external monologue*. Writing the desired external dialogue of your audience will allow you to pinpoint exactly what where you want your audience to be in your story. You can then construct, evaluate, and edit your conflict events to guide your audience through your story.

External dialogues can also be a good tool to see if your story is working the way you want it to. Once you have a working storyboard or animatic, have someone else write an external dialogue for you. Check it against what you desire for your piece. Where are the audience members getting lost or bored? Do they know the ending before you want them to? Look for places where they are thinking or feeling something different from what you want them to. When you find these places implement different tactics or reactions, compound the problem differently, or change the story structure to guide your audience to where you want them to be.

Building a Story: Questions to Ask Yourself:

1. Who is your character?

2. What is your character's goal?

3. What is your inciting moment?

4. Does your conflict rise?

5. What is your character's reaction (not action) to the conflict?

6. What does your character need to learn?

7. Does your ending relate to your beginning?

8. Is your audience entertained?

Summary

There is no magic formula for making a good story. Good story is a combination of strong character combined with the appropriate choice of structure, conflict, emotion, and reaction for that character. Knowing the options allow the storyteller to experiment, search, and find the best way to tell the story.

When building story, remember:

- The story will change. You are searching for the best way to tell the story. Consider the following on your search:
  - Character
  - Genre
  - Time and Place
  - Point of View

- When constructing the story, there are variations on structure that may work better for your situation:
  - Linear
  - Parallel
  - Circular
  - Bus-Stop
  - Ping-Pong or Zig-Zag
- Know your ending before you build plot points. Let your ending influence your beginning.
- When building conflict, remember that conflict occurs in patterns:
  - Compounded
  - Accumulated
- Conflict must rise in intensity.
- The character in conflict will try different tactics to resolve the conflict.
- The reaction of the character to the conflict is driven by thought and emotion. This is called *internal monologue*.
- The audience is also driven by thought and emotion. This is called *external monologue*.
- The audience will be in one of four places in relationship to the character and the story:
  - The character knows more than the audience
  - The audience learns as the character learns
  - The audience knows more than the character
  - The audience *thinks* it knows more than the character
- Successful storytelling requires the exploration of possibilities until you find the most entertaining way to tell the story.

Recommended Readings

1. Linda J. Cowgill, *Writing Short Films: Structure and Content for Screenwriters*

2. Robert McKee, *Story*

3. Jeffrey Scott, *How to Write for Animation*

4. James Mercurio, *Killer Endings*, DVD

Notes

[1] Stan Howard, *MakeMovies: AnimationScriptwriting*. http://www.makemovies.co.uk/.

[2] Stan Howard, *MakeMovies: AnimationScriptwriting*. http://www.makemovies.co.uk/. This structure is not a new idea, but I have not found the term *bus-stop* used in any other source.

[3]Stan Howard, *MakeMovies: AnimationScriptwriting. http://www.makemovies.co.uk/*. This structure is not a new idea, but I have not found the term *zig-zag* used in any other source.

[4]James Mercurio, *Killer Endings,* DVD, Screenwriting Expo Seminar Series #027, Creative Screenwriting Publications, Inc., Los Angeles, CA, 2006.

[5]Stan Howard, *MakeMovies: AnimationScriptwriting. http://www.makemovies.co.uk/*. Stan Howard lays out problem patterns as single events, domino effects, ripple effects, and global effects. He introduces the idea of Accumulated Conflict and Patterns of Problems on his website. His information was instrumental in rethinking the pattern of these problems in slightly different ways.

Story and Humor: An Interview with Chris Renaud and Mike Thurmeier, Blue Sky Animation Studios

Chris Renaud started in New York City, drawing for Marvel and DC Comics. In 2000, he was hired as an illustrator and then a production designer on *The Book of Pooh* and *Bear in the Big Blue House*, for the Disney Channel. After being production designer on *It's a Big, Big World*, for PBS, Chris was hired by Blue Sky. He started as a story artist on *Ice Age 2* and *Robots*, and then went to shorts. Chris was director with Mike Thurmeier on *No Time for Nuts*, winner of ASIFA's Annie Award for Best Animated Short and a nominee for the Academy Award for Best Animated Short Subject.

Mike Thurmeier has been an animator at Blue Sky since 1998, when he was hired out of Sheridan College with no formal animation training. He animated several Blue Sky commercials and feature film projects before serving as a lead animator and additional story artist on the company's first film, *Ice Age*. He was a supervising animator on Blue Sky's features, *Robots* and *Ice Age 2* and was senior supervising animator on *Horton Hears a Who*.

No Time for Nuts, **directed by Chris Renaud and Mike Thurmeier, Blue Sky Studios**

Q: How do you recognize a good idea for an animated short?

Chris: I think the way to recognize a good idea is to understand where we're starting, what the setup is, and how it's going to resolve. That may change as it goes through development, but I think that's how you recognize a good idea. Everything else is just a concept. What you'll often find, when you start with just a concept, is that you start going down a road and you'll find it doesn't go anywhere.

Mike: I find a good idea is one that I still like even after I've verbally pitched it to someone. Many times I'll sit and think about an idea, and think I've got it worked out, only to find as I'm actually telling someone about it I'm discovering the weaknesses or gaps in logic.

Q: What about the scope of the idea? Can you tell from knowing the set-up and how it resolves if it is too big?

Chris: Scale and scope have to do with how much money you have, how much time you have, and all that kind of stuff. When coming up with the idea for our short— obviously, I wanted Scrat to time travel—the question was, "How can we do it within the confines of our resources?" To conserve resources, we had Scrat go through time, running into humanity in various places but never actually showing humanity, to show flags being waved and arrows being shot, but never seeing any actual animated characters. That was the way that we could solve it within the confines of our production, not just budget, but time and everything.

For example, we're in the Roman Colosseum, rose petals come down, Scrat takes a bow, they're cheering him, and BOOM, he's hit by a chariot, and then the monster comes out.

In the short, we wanted to establish where we were, what the joke would be and then we're out.

Mike: It's a good rule of thumb to assume that most stories will get complicated just through the act of producing them, so it's better to start simple. I've also found that no matter how well you storyboard something, a character's performance will grow during the animation process, lengthening the film by a good amount.

Q: How do you build the plot points in between your beginning and your end?

Chris: That was the thing we struggled with the most. To me, and I think, to Mike, it has to do with pacing. Pacing is the language of filmmaking. And that doesn't mean going fast. It just means how you carry the audience from scene to scene. The pacing, at least in the case of a comedic short, must create an escalation. And for us, we just kept cutting ideas until we were tired, but it ended up being a solution that worked for us. The first segment when he's with the sword in the stone is the longest, and the Roman Colosseum was a little shorter, and the *Titanic* a little shorter, until they are very short bits leading right up to the statue of David—which was our big laugh—that was literally just a few frames.

Q: All of the Scrat films are humorous. How do you make them funny?

Chris: I feel like a lot of times humor becomes one of those weird things. It's like an innate sensibility to a certain degree, and everyone's a little different, but there are obvious ways to make things funny.

One good thing about Scrat is that the audience is going into the piece liking him and wanting to laugh. We are working with a known character. His design is great. Big goggle eyes help if you're designing a character for a short. To make things funny, relate-ability is a huge thing. Drawing on touchstones that your audience is familiar with on some level is a great way get some laughs. But put a twist on it.

Scrat is a classic physical comedy piece. Physical pain is the relatable element.

Even with physical pain, you have to try to set up the payoff. You can't just sit Scrat there and hit him on the head with a hammer. Hitting with a hammer has to mean something.

For example, with the sword in the stone moment, nothing painful happens to Scrat for a bit. At first he's very calm, then he finds the sword. When he draws the sword, there's a moment where he is heroic and for just an instant, you think maybe he is going to win this time. Of course, then the arrow comes in and things begin to go badly.

That turn is where the laugh comes. It's not the arrow coming in, it's the fact he's heroic and then he is not. Once we delivered that, then we could start doing physical pain in other events a bit more quickly, but you have to have the moment pay for itself.

In another example, Scrat shows up in the snow and he thinks he's home. Hopefully, the audience probably expects he's not home. Then you cut wide and you see a ship, the *Titanic*, coming through the mist. So there, the comedy of it is, "Oh, he's relieved, thank God it's over," and then the discovery that he is on the one piece of ice in history that actually is dangerous to be on. That ends up creating some laughs.

Mike: What makes the Scrat funny is equal parts situation and performance. The animation team has worked really hard to refine a handful of characteristics that really rely on timing; how fast does his head turn, how many times does he shift his eyes and blink, what kind of rhythm is there to his movement. How the Scrat reacts to a given situation is the key to his comedy. And the comedy of the Scrat films and shorts comes purely from his character; there's no dialogue or clever punch line.

Q: What advice would you give to students making their first short?

Chris: You need to create a character that you care about on some level and want to watch.

You just need to follow the principles of narrative. Have a beginning, middle, and end, and make it a manageable size, depending on your resources. You need to be able to make it. It's great to have an idea, but if you can't actually produce it, it's not worth the paper it's written on. So really think about what you can do within your skill set. If you're great at Flash, think within Flash. Know your strengths and your assets.

And I don't think you need to be completely unique because nothing is. You will always hear, "This is like that." It is always going to be the case because there are so many things out there and we are exposed to so much. That said, I think that you need to think of your spin on it and that will give it as much uniqueness as it needs.

Mike: I agree with Chris. You have to know what you want to make. Do you really want to make a complete short film that will make the festivals? Or, do you want a demo reel that showcases your specific area of expertise? If you're gunning to be an animator, it doesn't make sense to spend a ton of time modeling and lighting, only to have your animation side suffer.

But if you are going for a complete short film, it's all about quality over quantity. A half-finished, poorly executed epic won't get you as far as a high-quality shorter piece.

Chapter 6

The Purpose of Dialogue

Charlie Chaplin, Buster Keaton, The Roadrunner, and Wile E. Coyote (Chuck Jones) were masters of clarity of movement to communicate story without words. Often, animated shorts are devoid of dialogue because we don't necessarily need dialogue when we have the ability to exaggerate actions and reactions, push strong poses, and use visuals that are more powerful than words. In fact, we are always encouraged to show, don't tell.

However, there are times when your characters *need* to speak. The audience needs to hear what they have to say in order to maintain the suspension of disbelief, to communicate internal conflict, or to condense and drive the plot.

In Eric Drobile's *The Animator and the Seat,* as the chair grabs and pulls the escaping Chunk, the animator, from the bookcase and forces him back into the seat, Chunk cries out, "What do you want from me?!" It is exactly what all of us would do in his situation. If he did not speak at this moment, it would confuse the content. It helps to drive the plot forward. After this line of dialogue, the chair responds by showing Chunk exactly what it wants.

"What do you want from me?!" Eric Drobile, *The Animator and the Seat,* Ringling College of Art and Design

Other times it is the character's *goal* that requires speech. In *The ChubbChubbs,* the fumbling, good-hearted, helpful hero, Meeper, wants nothing more than to be a respected karaoke singer. In order to sing, he must also speak.

"Sock it to me! Sock it to me!"

"Why can't we be friends?"

"Hey Friends!"

"A little respect!"

The ChubbChubbs, directed by Eric Armstrong, Sony Pictures Imageworks

Sometimes it is not what you say, but how you say it. In *A Great Big Robot from Outer Space Ate My Homework,* Mark Shirra uses nonsense language that communicates both the desperation of the boy (Bertie Lated) and the disbelief of the teacher (Miss Spleen). Again, if they did not vocalize, it would be unbelievable. The whole point is trying to explain why Bertie doesn't have his homework. But what they say is not as important as the intonation, the pacing, and the passing of the dialogue between the characters.

Shirra said this about his dialogue: "The dialogue was meant to be largely *visceral* gobble-dygook with the occasional comprehensible word thrown in. When I recorded the voices, I pretty much made a lot of it up as I went along, but I had storyboard drawings to look at so I knew what needed to be said, even if in an abstract way!"

"Beep! Beep! Beep!"
Mark Shirra, *A Great Big Robot from Outer Space Ate My Homework*, Vancouver Film School

Similarly, the dialogue in Chris Nabholz's short, *Respire, Mon Ami,* is composed in French. It sets the mood of the piece. Intended for a primarily English-speaking audience, the subtitles create anticipation and suspense and control the timing of the release of information.

"Let me help you with that!"
Chris Nabholz, *Respire, Mon Ami*, Ringling College of Art and Design

The Purpose of Dialogue

In this chapter, we are going to define the functions that dialogue serves in a story so that you can choose when and how to use it well. Then we will see how these are put into practice in a dialogue analysis of the short script, *The Captain,* by Christianne Greiert and Nick Pierce.

Setting the Mood

A short can begin with dialogue:

- A mother singing a lullaby
- A man yelling at the top of his lungs
- Children telling jokes, playing, and laughing
- A bank teller counting money

All of these things could almost be defined as ambient sound—the same as wind through the trees, or cars and sirens in a city—except for the fact that *what* the mother is singing, *what* the man is yelling, *which* jokes the children are telling, *how* much money is being counted *should* have specific meaning that drives the plot forward, foreshadows the theme of the piece, or establishes a story question. How can a good mother sing Heavy Metal to her newborn infant? The man is yelling *HELP!* What does he need and will he get it? Where did little children like *that* learn jokes like *those?!*

Sometimes dialogue can change the mood. Perhaps there is a boxing match on the TV in a bar. As two men begin to fight over a seat at the bar, the boxing match escalates and the voice of the sports announcer seems to be narrating the conflict of the men in the bar instead. The point is that everything that is said in your piece, whether it is background or foreground information, has meaning. What we hear as background information can also set the mood.

Revealing the Character

When dialogue reveals the character it means that what the character says discloses his or her goals, personality, needs, fears, and transformation.

There are four main ways that dialogue reveals character:

1. It reveals a character's goal or motivation.
   Robber: "Money will fix everything."

2. It reveals a character's attitude toward a situation.
   Robber: "Isn't it a little late for this?"

3. It reveals the antagonist's motive.
   Robber: "No one told me there were four guards."

4. It can reveal a character's transformation over time.
Robber: "Maybe tomorrow."

Driving the Plot Forward

When dialogue drives the plot, it does so by acting on the train of thought and emotions of the audience or reveals information to the character that forces him or her to act.

There are five main ways that dialogue drives the plot forward:

1. Creates curiosity
Robber #1: "Did you bring it?"

2. Creates tension (through the exchange of power—social, political, sexual, or physical)
Robber #1: "Are you sure *you* picked the right place?"

3. Creates conflict by presenting new information
Robber #2: "No, I'm not sure. My mother would be so disappointed in me."

4. Shows us something we did not expect
Police: "We're here to check on a disturbance."

5. Builds suspense for what is to come
Bank Teller: "We'll be closing in 10 minutes."
Robber #1: "What now?"

Driving the Resolution

When dialogue drives the resolution it implies, reinforces, or reveals the theme of the piece. Review the section on themes in Chapter 1. Remember how often, in films, the characters remind us of the theme of the piece through dialogue.

Robber #2: "Getting a job would be easier than this!"

Creating Subtext

Subtext always seems like a difficult concept. But if you link it to emotion it becomes relatively easy. One of the biggest pitfalls of dialogue is that beginning writers mirror exactly what the character is thinking with what they are saying. Don't do this.

At the beginning of *The Animator and the Seat*, Chunk is tired and needs a break. He doesn't say, "I'm so tired. I think I'll take a break." Instead the audience sees mounds of soda cans and empty coffee pots (not cups . . . pots!). Chunk sighs, "I used to like bears."

And the audience is given the opportunity to view what he has been forced to spend hours animating. His simple phrase, coupled with the visuals, communicates it all in a much more powerful way. He *is* tired. He *does* need a break. But we don't have to hit the audience over the head with the message.

"I used to like bears."
Eric Drobile, *The Animator and the Seat*, Ringling College of Art and Design

As human beings we rarely, if confusingly, say exactly what we think—and this is because of emotion. Remember that in story, our characters are in conflict and there is something at stake. Therefore, emotions run high. Characters tend not to say what they think because it is either a) too risky or rude to say what they really think or b) the other party already knows what they think.

Let's review our acting situation from Chapter 3 and watch this exchange again on the DVD. The dialogue is benign, but the internal monologues of our characters are emotionally charged.

Dialogue	Internal Monologue
A: Hello.	I am so happy to see you. I miss you so much. I hope this goes well. Please be pleased to see me too!
B: Hello.	I can't believe I agreed to meet you. Don't look like such a puppy dog!
A: How are you?	Oh no. She doesn't seem receptive. But she's here. Maybe I have a chance.
B: Fine.	This is a mistake. How do I make him go away?
A: Really?	She doesn't want me here.
B: Yes.	No.

This is subtext. Subtext, in dialogue, is saying one thing, but meaning another. We understand the true meaning of the words through the situation, intonation, and the physical interaction and gestures of the characters.

Using Narration

Every time a narrator speaks, it is like interrupting the story. Make sure that everything that is said is carefully chosen to move the plot forward and/or condense time without confusing the viewer or giving away too much information. You want to make sure that there is a balance between your narration and your visuals. Too often, the visuals become an illustration of the narration. You can remove the visuals and still have the complete story. We work in a visual medium. The narration must support but not dominate the visuals. If you find yourself in this situation, find another execution for your story—or maybe find another story.

There is a difference between narration and voiceover. In *Forrest Gump*, we have narration that reveals the inner thoughts of the character as he looks back on his life. In *Poor Bogo*, we have voiceover that adds another dimension to the situation of our storybook character as we *hear* one conflict, but watch another.

"After all his adventures, Bogo was so tired he went right to sleep...."

"Oh no daddy, Bogo is not sleepy, he is HUNGRY!"
Thelvin Cabezas, *Poor Bogo*, Ringling College of Art and Design

Tempo, Pacing, Rhythm, Intonation, and Timing

Early in the chapter, we looked at the use of dialogue in *A Great Big Robot from Outer Space Ate My Homework* and *Respire, Mon Ami*. Because they use other languages, they are good examples of tempo, pacing, rhythm, intonation, and timing of the dialogue in relationship to the content and emotion of the piece.

Listen to them. Try to graph the rise and fall of the intonation of the voices. Pay attention to pacing and rhythm of what the actors are saying as the conflict rises. Focus on the *silences* in the scene. Silence can punctuate a line of dialogue, enhancing both the emotion and impact of what is said. Silence allows your audience time to comprehend what your characters are saying. Silence allows time for other characters to react. Too often, beginning animators seem to fear silence when creating dialogue. They do too much too quickly and without time for the dialogue to support the emotion of the scene.

When creating dialogue, write down what you want your characters to say. Then record it a number of different ways. Take the script away and improvise the dialogue. Have many different people do it for you. If you are lucky enough to have a college or theater in your area, see if you can hire an actor to improvise your dialogue for you. It is amazing how much the voice and interpretation of the words can enhance your animation and help you determine the extremes of your poses.

Notes on Music and Sound

Music and sound do not play the same role as dialogue. As Sonia Moore said, "The words are like toy boats on the water." They reveal the underbelly of the emotion of the character. And sometimes, if the acting is good, the words are irrelevant.

Music and sound, however, play the role of a supporting character. If you do not pay as much attention to the development of the music and sound as you do to the development of your story and hero, it can make or break your piece.

For every footstep, glass clink, pencil tap, or rain-on-the-window element of your piece that makes noise, you must find or create that noise. You must also create the sound of the environment, the ambient sounds of nature, city, fluorescent lights in an office, and diners in a restaurant. There are many copyright-free sounds available on DVD and on the Internet. Make sure that your sound is copyright-free and that it is truly the right sound for your piece. If you need the bark of a German shepherd, don't compromise or substitute the bark of a greyhound. Someone will know the difference and it will break your suspension of disbelief.

Too often, beginning animators are more interested and experienced in image-making than in creating sound and music. They will find a piece of copyright-free music that fits the rhythm and pacing of their animation and lay it underneath the visuals. Simply finding music that matches the pacing of the piece is not enough. The music must mirror and support the emotional rise and fall, the intensity of the rising conflict as the piece progresses. If it does not, the music flattens those moments and can actually do more harm than good.

The very best thing to do is compose custom music. If you are not good at composing music, find someone to do it for you. As much as you need to get your animation out there to help your career, musicians and actors need to get their talents out there as well. Usually for a nominal fee, credit, and a copy of the finished piece (with permission to distribute on their portfolio), you can find people to help you.

Dialogue Analysis of *The Captain*

We can find almost all of the purposes of dialogue except narration in this script for an animated short, *The Captain*.

Script: *The Captain* by Christianne Greiert and Nick Pierce	Purpose of Dialogue

LOCKER ROOM SCENE
Characters: Coach
          Charlie
          Max
Concept: There is no "I" in T-E-A-M
Premise: Charlie, the team captain of the Fighting Cobras, has a knee injury that will keep him from playing in the championship game. He must learn what it truly means to be a leader.
FADE IN.
INT. FIGHTING COBRAS HIGH SCHOOL LOCKER ROOM	

Script: *The Captain* by Christianne Greiert and Nick Pierce	Purpose of Dialogue
Two players sit on benches near their lockers suiting up for the big game. The wall to the front is lined with school banners and pennants from years gone by. There is a trophy case with only two trophies and a series of team pictures. Off screen there is a band playing, crowds cheering. We hear cheerleaders chanting "T-E-A-M. Gooooo TEAM!"	*Exposition:* "Go Team!" Establishes the theme, sets the mood of the piece
COACH: **(Clapping his hands excitedly)** All Right! All Right! Ten minutes till game time, men. Everything you've got—put it on the field tonight! Coach and most of the team exit except for Charlie and Max. Charlie is only half-dressed, while Max laces and unlaces his shoes. Max is stalling.	The coach plays the role of the herald, bringing information to the story. This inserts the narrator into the story without breaking the story.
CHARLIE: **(Sitting in a warm-up suit with a towel around his shoulders)** Nervous? **MAX:** Um . . . not really.	Sets mood, establishes emotion of characters.
CHARLIE: **(Standing up quickly)** You should be. We've been waiting for a championship for the last four seasons. Charlie opens his locker, tossing his towel inside. He is clearly irritated.	Reveals character. Establishes external goal.
MAX: **(Finishing tying his shoelaces)** OK, what's crawled up your shorts, dude? **CHARLIE:** Nothing. I'm just saying this is a big deal and you need to be ready.	*Inciting Moment:* Drives plot. Establishes internal conflict.
MAX: I'm ready . . . You know, I didn't choose to start. **CHARLIE:** Well, I didn't choose to bust my knee, either. Life's not fair—not today at least. Hangs up the towel and starts to straighten the things in his locker. **MAX:** Is that your idea of a team captain's pep talk?	*Conflict:* Drives plot. Heightens conflict.
CHARLIE: Nope, not doing it.	Reveals Charlie's role.
MAX: So you don't get to play and it's "forget about the rest of us"? We've all worked for— Charlie slams his locker door.	Reveals character. Reveals character. Drives plot.
CHARLIE: All I can do is cross my fingers and hope some second-string sophomore doesn't screw it up.	

Script: *The Captain* by Christianne Greiert and Nick Pierce	Purpose of Dialogue
MAX: Whoa! What's wrong with you? Before you, when a soccer ball flew at my head —I actually ducked. And now, when all I want is to do half as well as you could, you cut me down? Thanks. Coach reappears, clipboard and playbook in hand.	
COACH: All right guys, game time. We've been working for this all season. OK, Max, you loose? **(Starts to rub MAX's shoulders)** Warm? Feeling quick on your feet? Remember, the left side of the defense —there are some holes there.	Breaks tension. Allows plot to stay on course. Refocuses on the game.
MAX: Yeah, I got it Coach. **(to CHARLIE)** I've got some warm-ups to do. See you out there. Max exits throwing Charlie a disdainful look. Charlie turns back toward his locker. None of this gets past the coach, who sighs and shakes his head.	Subtext
COACH: Charlie, I hope you've got some words of wisdom for these boys. They need it. See you on the sidelines. Coach pats Charlie with the playbook and exits.	Drives resolution.
CHARLIE: (Punching his fist into a locker) Aargh! What the hell am I going to do now? No speech. No knee. No hope for a trophy. After four years—this is not how I thought it would end. Coach reappears.	*Crisis Moment:* Drives the plot.
COACH: Charlie, will you get out here? This punk of a sophomore goalie won't start until you're there. He's saying he needs your blessing or something like that. **CHARLIE:** What?	Drives resolution.
COACH: You're still the captain, Charlie. Get out there and act like it.	*Climax:* Drives resolution. Reveals theme. Throws Charlie into his point of no return. He must make a choice.
Charlie watches as the door slams behind the coach. Grabbing his jersey, he pulls it on as he limps out the door. END SCENE **FADE OUT**	*Resolution:* And we celebrate.

Exercise: *The Captain* was written for a group project. If you were working alone, how could you condense the role of the coach into the character of Max? How could you alter what Max says to serve the same purpose?

Exercise: On first read, *The Captain* would appear to be better for live action than for animation. Brainstorm visuals that would make animation the necessary medium for this story.

Summary

Dialogue serves the following purposes:

- Sets the mood of the piece
- Reveals the character
- Drives the plot forward
- Drives the resolution
- Creates subtext

There are two things to watch out for when you use narration:

- It can interrupt the story and break the flow of your piece.
- It is easy to "illustrate" the narration rather than create unique visuals with meaning of their own.

Music and sound need to be treated as supporting characters to the story.

- Too often new animators use music and sound as filler instead of carefully building sound and music to support the content and rising conflict of the piece.

Often animated shorts do not have dialogue. There are times when your characters have to speak in order to be truthful to the story. Understanding how dialogue functions allows you, as a storyteller, to use it well.

Recommended Readings

1. Linda Seger, *Creating Unforgettable Characters*, Chapter 1: Writing Dialogue.

2. Will Eisner, *Graphic Storytelling*.

3. Gloria Kempton, *Dialogue: Techniques and Exercises for Crafting Effective Dialogue*.

4. Robin Beauchamp, *Designing Sound for Animation*.

Notes

The purpose of dialogue in this chapter comes from a condensation of the sources above coupled with experience working with beginning animators to develop story. It doesn't cover everything about dialogue, but provides the basics necessary to begin. Use the sources above if you find you need to go deeper.

Pitching Stories: Sande Scoredos, Sony Pictures Imageworks

Sande Scoredos is the executive director of training and artist development at Sony Pictures Imageworks. She is committed to working with academia, serving on school advisory boards, guiding curriculum, participating on industry panels, and lecturing at school programs. She was instrumental in founding the Imageworks Professional Academic Excellence (IPAX) program in 2004. Sande chaired the SIGGRAPH 2001 Computer Animation Festival and is the curator chair for the SIGGRAPH 2008 Computer Animation Festival.

Sande produced *Early Bloomer*, a short film that was theatrically released. Her other credits include: *Stuart Little, Hollow Man, Spider Man, Stuart Little 2, I Spy, Spider-Man 2, Full Spectrum Warrior, The Polar Express, Open Season, Spider-Man 3,* and *Surf's Up.* Currently in production are *Beowulf, I Am Legend, Watchman, Cloudy with a Chance of Meatballs.*

Before the Pitch: Register Your Work

Before you pitch your idea to anyone, including your family, friends, your uncle Joe who works at a studio, or even to random strangers, protect everyone—and your idea—by finding out who owns the rights to your idea. Do not talk about your idea until you have gone through the registration process or have an agent. You never know who is listening at Starbuck's. If you are pitching for a school project, you may find that your school already owns the rights. Likewise, if you work in the entertainment industry, your company may own the rights to anything resembling intellectual property. Ask your career services advisor or legal department about ownership rights and be sure to read your deal memo and contract agreement.

Most studios will only take pitch meetings through an agent. That is to protect you and them against copyright claims. For information on copyright filings, check the United States Copyright Office website, *http://www.copyright.gov/*. Read the guidelines carefully and follow the procedures.

Know Who Will Hear Your Pitch

Now, prepare for that pitch.

Successful pitches are carefully designed and orchestrated. Many brilliant ideas have fallen by the wayside due to poor pitching skills.

Whether you are pitching a 30-second short to your animation professor or an epic to a studio executive, *find out who is going to hear your pitch.*

You have just a few seconds to grab their attention and convince everyone in the room that your story is worth telling. How you describe it, visualize it, sell it, and sell yourself can all work for you or against you.

First, be honest and decide if you are the best person to make the pitch. If you get flustered speaking to a group, then let someone else do the talking. Not everyone needs to be part of the formal presentation so play to your strengths.

Talk to the "gatekeeper," a key contact who is setting up the meeting and ask him or her to tell you who might attend. If you can, find out their titles and what influence they have on the process. Then do your homework.

The World Wide Web is a wealth of information. Check out the backgrounds of each person who may be in the meeting.

- Try to get a recent picture of each person.
- What types of projects do they like?
- What projects have they worked on?
- Where did they grow up?
- What college did they attend?
- What projects are in their catalog? Do they already have an animated film about two talking zebras? Oops, your project is about two zebras so think about how your project fits into their plans.
- Get your facts straight and then double-check them. Just because it is on the web or IMDB does not make it true.

Why is this important? If you can find a relevant personal connection, then you can tap into that with a casual chat, discover mutual acquaintances or interests. But be careful. You want to stand out just a little more from the other pitches and be remembered in a good way. Your pitch should always be short and to the point, not too deep or detailed, or it can get boring. You want a balance of well rehearsed but not memorized, engaging, and delivered with enthusiasm but not clownish and with confidence and passion for the project.

This business is all about relationships, so you want to connect with the people in the room.

Preparing for the Pitch

Make sure you know your story. Research your idea and know what else is out there that remotely resembles it. Is there a character, city, situation, movie, or game that is similar to yours? You can bet that someone at the pitch will say this sounds like "XYZ," the classic film from 1932 directed by some obscure foreign director. Assume that anyone in the pitch session has seen it and heard it all. Nothing is worse than the silence you hear that follows the comment, "What else have you got?" A potentially embarrassing moment can turn in your favor if you can intelligently discuss the other work, and its relationship to yours. You will look good if you not only know of this piece but also can intelligently discuss this reference.

You also want to make sure you have the rights to the properties and characters. Say your story centers around a landmark building in downtown New York. Believe it or not, you may not be able to obtain or afford the rights to use the building. The same goes for characters and music. If your story cannot be made without that specific Beatles song, consider the reality and cost of acquiring the rights.

If your project requires getting the rights, be prepared to discuss the status of your negotiations in the meeting. If you do not have an original concept and cannot afford to obtain rights for existing properties, check out the properties in the public domain.

Read the industry trade publications to see what types of projects are going into production. If there is something similar to your proposal, then you should be able to address any concerns about copyright infringement up front and explain what makes your idea better. Let the people hearing the pitch initiate talk about what actors or other talent would be good for the project.

Pitch the Entertainment Value

You can show you are looking at the whole package by suggesting the entertainment value, genre, audience age, and appeal of your project. Describe the concept by giving a general sense of the visuals for the characters, environments, and style. Use sketches, color drawings, color palettes, reference material, special lighting, video clips—anything that will get the visuals across. Sometimes you can get into the room early to stage the pitch. This is another benefit to knowing the "gatekeeper." Remember, you are pitching to people who hear dozens of ideas and you want them to remember your project. If you can entertain them, they will see you can entertain audiences too.

Be ready to answer questions about finances and marketability since there may be financial people at the pitch.

At the Pitch

Remember that your pitch starts the minute you arrive—in the parking lot or in the elevator—you never know who you might run into so be nice to everyone. Once in the room, have a friendly handshake, thank them all for meeting with you, and tell them you admire their work. Show them by your posture, body language and demeanor that you are enthusiastic and excited. Don't be overly intense. Get everyone's name in the room and try to identify the leader, but don't forget to make eye contact with each of them.

You need to conquer the whole room. Dress appropriately and watch your language. Listen to all the ideas and suggestions with openness and encourage suggestions. Show them how you work with others.

After the Pitch

Have a closing prepared. Never end your pitch with "Well, that's it" or "So, what do you think?" End with a positive note and thank them again, emphasizing how much you want to work with them. Ask them if they have any suggestions and show your willingness to make adjustments.

It helps to have some sort of "leave behind" object, something more creative than a business card or demo reel. For a story about dogs, maybe a small stuffed animal with a creative dog tag containing your contact information and the name of the project.

Within a week, follow up with the gatekeeper to see if you can get a pulse on the interest in your project.

Handwritten thank you notes are welcome but emails usually are not. Keep track of everyone you pitch with a journal; track names, dates, titles, and contact information. Selling your idea is really about relationships and at the end of the pitch, you want everyone in the room wanting to work with you and to feel confident that your project is their next winner.

Chapter 7

Storyboarding

Above drawing and the rest, the greatest single attribute of a successful story artist is imagination. Applying imagination to storyboarding is easier said than done but ultimately the imaginative storyteller will see more of their work on the screen. Movies, comics, graphic novels, and Manga are great starting points to see what others are doing, but the goal is originality.

Barry Cook, Animator, former Disney Story Development artist,
and Director of Disney's *Mulan*

Storyboards are a way for the filmmaker to pre-visualize the film-story as a series of still drawings in order to chart visual flow and continuity as well as to plan for stylistic integrity and story clarity. Storyboarding is a blueprint and a way of visualizing the whole of your film by depicting its individual shots. In larger productions, this blueprint is an essential form of communication to the many artists and technicians who need to know what is expected in the film. The storyboards for a film are not usually seen by the public, but their importance in making a story idea visual for film is vital. Storyboards need to capture the essence of an image's storytelling power. Learn to recognize powerful storytelling images.

I saw this situation on my way home from work one day. I didn't see the accident but I did not have to ask, "What happened?" The image tells the whole story.

Drawing

Storyboards are created to plan one's own film. Other times they are created in collaboration with story teams to "work out" and realize how a film is going to play. These "process boards" can be simple thumbnails one creates to keep things ordered. Scribbles, stick figures with words, diagrams, and arrows may suffice as long as everyone who needs to know what is going on can understand their meaning. "Presentation storyboards," on the other hand, are made to show others how the film is expected to look. Presentation boards may need to be drawn well enough to be understood by people who are not artists or filmmakers. Presentation boards carry information about style and content of the film. One may need to create a sense of volume, structure, and weight in the drawing but detail is not usually important. Simplicity and clarity are important. Frank Gladstone, a 35-year animation veteran, Producer and Training Director at several major animation studios including Disney, DreamWorks, and Warner Brothers, said, "I actually find that finely detailed boards are often difficult to read. Better to be clear than polished."

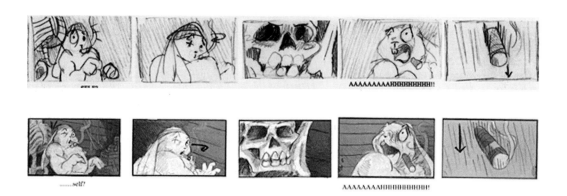

Visual Imagination

Those who have learned to draw well have not trained their fingers so much as they have trained their minds. Drawing requires heightened visual powers. Those who draw well are usually more able to visualize and imagine images and are obviously more capable of communicating their vision to others. Those who struggle with drawing sometimes struggle with visual ideas and have difficulty illustrating those ideas clearly.

It is important that the storyboard artist can show form and descriptive detail with clarity. The ability to draw varied perspectives and spatial relationships is also critical. Storyboard drawings need to communicate specific and often complex angles and action. Drawings of humans and other characters must move and act and be believable. Drawings of landscapes, architecture, machines, props, and natural elements such as wind and water may be required. It certainly helps if you love to draw and are fairly good at it.

Animation Storyboards

Despite the advances in technology for animation production, animation is usually a slow, labor-intensive process. Shots lasting a few seconds can take months to execute. Unlike live-action films, animation editing is mostly done up front. Animation shots need to be carefully planned so you know what you want to see in the film before many hours are invested in creating it. Storyboarding is how this planning is done. Good animation storyboards also propel the entire process by inspiring the other artists in the production pipeline. Storyboard drawings of action poses, facial expressions, and environments may become the first "key poses" of an animator's scene or suggest background and layout possibilities.

Animation, Action, and Exaggeration

Pushing action is the essence of animation and of storyboarding. The drawing has to "emote" as much as the animation and more since it doesn't move around.

Jim Story, former Disney Feature Animation story artist and instructor of story,
University of Central Florida

Much more than live-action, animation storyboard drawings often need to show exaggeration and caricature. Animated characters can move at lightning speed or have their eyes pop out of their heads, perform impossible physical feats, and defy gravity. The storyboard artist is bound only by his or her imagination and ability to draw. Animators have been making animals talk and characters fly long before the live-action guys figured out how to do it. Even something as primitive as Pat Sullivan's first animated short of Felix the Cat (1919 "Feline Folies") shows Felix pull musical notes out of the air and make them into a scooter on which he rides away. Today and in the future, digital film technology will be providing more choices to every aspect of film, so limitations keep disappearing for the filmmaker. This is where the storyboard artist's creative vision can excel.

Professional Story Artist

Can you express a series of thoughts visually? To be a successful storyboard artist, you need an overworking brain and plenty of imagination—you need to understand acting and staging, mood and lighting. You must be able to write dialogue and create characters. A storyboard artist creates the blueprint for the film. Storyboarding is the foundation of a film—a building will not stand without a solid foundation.

Nathan Greno, Walt Disney Feature Animation Storyboard Artist
and Story Supervisor

Professional storyboard artists are a rather small group. However, there is always a need for good storyboard artists because the heart of a good animated film and many live-action films comes from the visual telling of the story by the hands and imagination of a storyboard artist. Putting the story idea into visual form requires the skills and sensitivities of a filmmaker, a graphic artist, a storyteller, and an actor. Of course it doesn't hurt to have a fair understanding of animation, layout and set design, music, dance, comedy, and psychology. Large studios will invest many millions of dollars to make an animated film. These studios need good story artists and storyboard artists. All the money will not guarantee a good film. It requires a great story and a great telling of the story and that's what the story artists help to do.

Film Language and Cinematography

Even though you may be drawing with a pencil or on a computer tablet you are working to create a film (or a film-like video, digital or computer game story). This requires that you know how films and film-stories are constructed. The thousands of existing films, advertisements, music videos, and video games form a library of good, bad, and so-so filmmaking. It is important to learn how and why the most effective films work. Learn how filmmakers make the viewers understand complex plots and actions as well as the flow and timing of simpler scenes. Analyze what the filmmaker has done to make you feel the tension and fear, joy, triumph so that you laugh, cry, and squirm in your seat in all the right places. It is not only the fact that the evil zombie is hiding in the closet but it is how the director chooses to reveal this information to the audience that can make us shudder, snicker, or yawn.

A novelist may want you to hear the voice inside a character's head telling us how jealous and irrational he is. A filmmaker may choose to convey the same thing through lighting and camera angle. An animator can use deep and shallow space, strong poses, and maybe symbolic or referential images such as blazing fire or strong colors. All of these types of images and the way they are put together are the "language" of the film. Become a student of film. Analyze the filmmaker's choices. Imagine what changes you would make. See if the film has storyboard examples and other useful information in the supplements section of a DVD. Start a journal, do quick drawings of shots, and make other notes as you notice interesting things while watching movies. You will not be able to see a film quite the same way you did before you undertook this journey. However, you will be a better storyboard artist and you will probably find even more reasons to enjoy the films you watch.

Cinematography

Cinematography refers primarily to the photographic camera work of filmmaking. In live action the cinematographers are responsible for getting the right shot for the director. Similarly, the storyboard artist needs to "get the right shot" or at least draw the best approximation of that shot so that it becomes clear how that shot will work in the film. In animation, such things as light quality, a camera's focus, and camera effects like a lens' flair may be drawn or created artificially, through digital devices. The more you are aware of the possibilities of photography and cinematography the better storyboard artist you will be.

Single Shot to Sequence of Shots

A single image or shot possesses a certain amount of energy. A series of images will manipulate the flow of that energy. It can build to a crescendo or stop us in our tracks. It can tease us, irritate us, make us feel the monotony of a long wait or the excitement of an unexpected surprise. This kind of energy comes from the kinds of pictures you create and the sequence and pace at which they are presented.

A picture that shows something we recognize will carry a large portion of the message and the energy of your story, such as a crying face, a hand reaching for a gun, or an empty chair. Beyond the subject, the storyboard artist must also consider *how* the subject is presented in each shot and sequence of shots. I am referring to the visual design. Balance, shape, line, space, tone, color, and texture are elements of visual design and are tools of the storyboard artist. These formal, abstract elements speak more directly to our emotions and cause us to feel a certain way about any subject. The evolution of design elements through a sequence can echo the thematic and emotional changes in your story. It can start with a single image, perhaps an empty chair. After all, an empty chair can make us feel like we are lonely and miss someone who is not there or it can be inviting us to sit down and join in on the activities. It may say that someone has just left or that someone is expected. A storyboard artist needs to consider what idea is being communicated and create a design for the shot that sends that message to our emotions. The juxtaposition of one shot to the one before and after can reshape the idea and further condition our reaction. It is the art of knowing what to show and how you show it.

Formal Elements of Visual Design

If you create a scene that shows a landscape with rolling hills and slow undulating horizontal curves, it may suggest a feeling of peacefulness. A shot of a rocky mountain cliff with jagged, pointed shapes might make us feel danger and tension. Certain colors can evoke excitement. Deep and shallow space can make us feel free or claustrophobic. The juxtaposition of these elements can provoke even more heightened emotional responses. There are many good art books about design. Find some and study the principles of design for their own sake. However, it is important to understand how to use these principles to tell stories in film. One of my favorite books on this topic is Bruce Block's *The Visual Story*. Remember that you cannot separate what you are showing us from the way you use the formal elements of design to convey an image's emotional content.

Soft rounded shapes may seem inviting and comfortable, while straight harsh edges may seem cold and impersonal.

Thumbnailing

Pre-Visualizing the Pre-Visualization

All the storyboard artists I have interviewed, without exception, said they do thumbnails in the early stages of the boarding process. Most every designer or graphic artist uses small thumbnail drawings as the first step to arriving at an image. Why? Because they are quick and rough. You may have several versions of an image in mind so you need to "get them out" and down on a piece of paper to compare and evaluate. In other cases, an artist may have no clear image in mind so he or she develops it on the paper, maybe even placing things randomly at first in order to start to see the possibilities for a shot and to consider how a series of shots work together.

Approaches to Thumbnailing

During thumbnailing, one can be experimental, daring, and perhaps even careless. They can let their mind and vision flow without feeling restrictions or the stifling influence of practical concerns. Sometime the most creative ideas come when you are not worried about being sensible or pragmatic. These early investigations usually have to be adjusted or even thrown out but they can help you conjure up possibilities. Another approach would be to start arranging basic images in an order that seems to follow the simplest and most direct depiction of the narrative. This approach may not produce the most exciting and adventurous results at first, but it may disclose to the storyboard artist a kind of "skeleton structure" upon which more innovative solutions may be built. It is important to be open-minded, imaginative, and flexible. No matter how rough, primitive, or even ugly these drawings may be, they are the first step toward realizing your film.

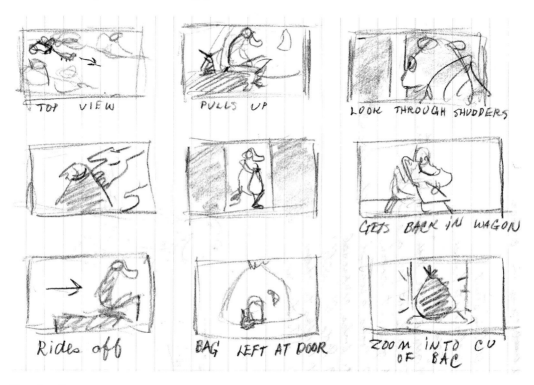

Thumbnails

Beat Sheet

A beat is one of the smallest elements of a film. It is a single event, action, or visual image. Story artists and filmmakers often choose to write out a beat-by-beat description of what will happen in a scene. This is a good way to let the narrative concepts of a story start to form pictures and shots in the imagination of the storyteller.

1. A shot of the outside of a grass hut village.

2. A wagon and driver comes down the road.

3. He stops in front of one of the huts.

4. Inside the house, a mouse is looking out of a gap in the shuttered window.

5. Wagon driver takes a sack from the back of his wagon.

6. Driver leaves the bag on the doorstep and rides away.

Shot List

In addition to a beat sheet, you may also have a shot list. A shot list takes the beat sheet to the next level. A shot list starts to anticipate the cinematic form the beats will take. The shot list will explain how it will look on film by describing every individual shot. A beat, which say—a wagon and driver come down the road, could be one shot or a half-dozen different shots depending on how the filmmaker wanted to present this action.

1. Extreme long high-angle shot of village with a driver and wagon already in scene.

2. Cut to closer shot from same camera angle as wagon slows in front of a particular hut.

3. Medium over-shoulder shot of wagon driver looking at chosen hut.

4. Close-up ¾ back view as mouse cracks open shutters and looks through the gap.

5. Close-up of a hand reaching for a dark cloth bag in the back of the wagon.

6. Handheld camera shot from mouse's point of view through the shutters of the driver carrying the bag toward the house.

7. Front view medium shot of driver getting back in his wagon.

8. Same view as driver grabs reins and motions to go.

9. Same view of wagon leaving frame, revealing bag at front door.

10. Camera zooms slowly toward the bag.

11. Close-up of bag.

A filmmaker may choose to develop beat sheets and shot lists for the entire film. If you are doing a short this may be a very good idea. These devices can be used to help realize your vision and can be very valuable, but these lists do not necessarily represent the final version of the film. You should approach them as preliminary plans, subject to change.

Draw and Change

If you give a beat sheet to 10 people you are probably going to have at least 10 different versions of how these shots will look. Written and spoken words are not specific enough. You need to make drawings. Imagine your images playing like a film. Ask yourself, "Can they be made better, more interesting?" "How do I want the audience to feel; worried, suspicious, or indifferent?" "Who or what is the center of attention in this shot?" The answers to some of these questions may evolve as a series of images develop. You may be many hours into a project before the best solutions begin to reveal themselves. Revisions will certainly be needed. From shots to scenes to sequences to acts to a finished film, it is important to see the flow of images as malleable and open to reinvention.

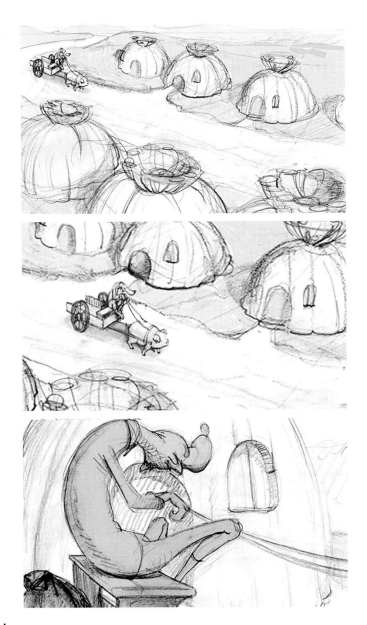

Finished boards

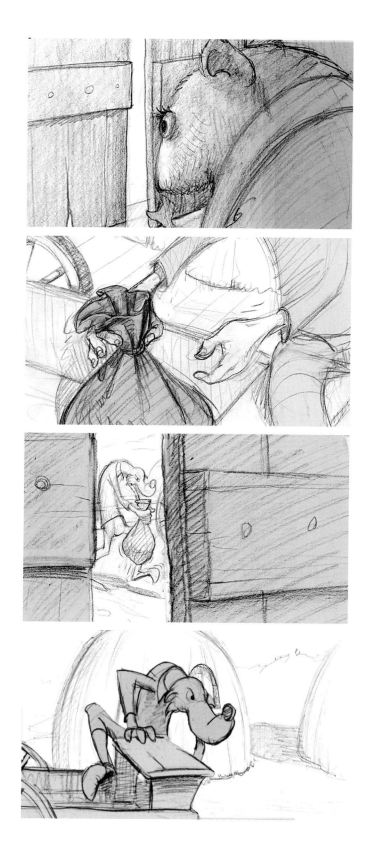

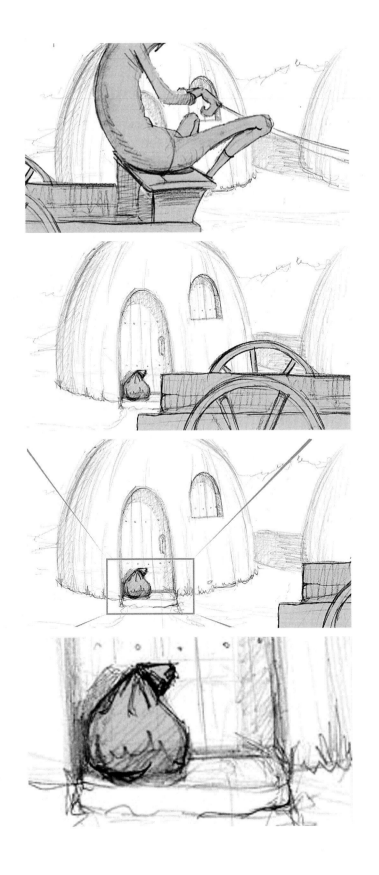

Continuity

Continuity refers to the logical flow and consistency of the images. Your audience's suspension of disbelief will be lost if they notice a continuity problem. This can pertain to a number of things such as the appearance of objects, the lighting, or direction of movement. The viewer will be confused if things are changed too much or are changed illogically from one cut to the next. If the light is casting shadows to the left in the first shot, don't switch them to the right when returning to the original camera angle. If a baseball dugout is left of the batter's mound, do not show the batters coming up to home plate from the right. The storyboards serve as a guide for the film; they need to be correct to prevent later problems. It is advisable for artists to create diagrams and floor plans of a space in order to keep the position of things from various angles clear and logical. If it is not completely clear for the storyboard artist, it may not be clear for the viewer.

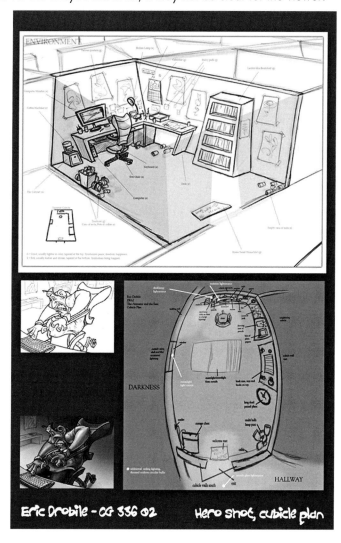

Eric Drobel's environment plans

180-Degree Rule

Steve Gordon, professional storyboard artist for Disney and DreamWorks, said, "I've seen some student storyboards and some test storyboards from non-students. What seems to be most lacking is the understanding of basic cinematography, screen direction, and why a scene should cut. Don't get me wrong, I also see some of these things in professional boards as well. The most important thing to learn is the 180-degree rule and how to work around it."

A common "slip-up" in storyboarding and film planning is continuity of movement or screen direction. If a train is moving from left to right on the screen, that train needs to continue moving left to right and not switch direction. If one were to do a cut where the camera appeared to have moved to the other side and the train was now moving from right to left, this could be disorienting for the audience. The audience may feel that they are now looking at a different train or perhaps this is now another time and place. This kind of cut is said to be breaking the 180-degree rule. The 180-degree rule is a guide to maintain a consistent positioning within the two-dimensional frame of the movie.

If two characters, say an armadillo and a frog, are playing "tug-o-war," a frog may be seen on the right facing left pulling on the rope. An armadillo may be seen on the left facing right pulling on the rope. The rope represents the 180-degree line. If the camera stays on the same side of that line, the frog will always be on the right and the armadillo will always be on the left even if the camera is shooting down the rope from one end of the action. If the camera crosses the 180-degree line and starts filming from the other side it will reverse the position of the frog and armadillo. The armadillo will then be on the right and the frog will be on the left. Again, this kind of reversal can confuse the audience. So the camera should not cross the 180-degree line or, to put it another way, you should avoid reversing the position or direction of your characters.

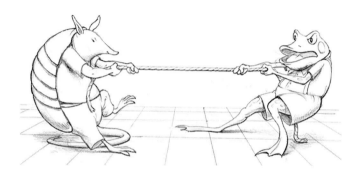

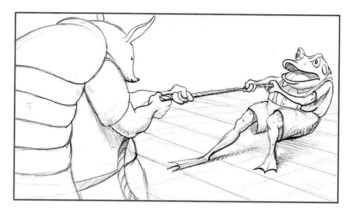

"Yes"

"Yes"

"This is breaking the 180-degree rule"

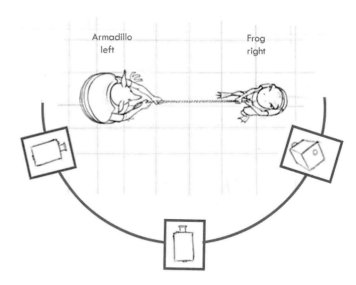

"Diagram of Cameras"

During a fast-action chase or other action scenes, the issue of screen direction may seem inconsequential but it probably is not. One could have an overhead shot of a horseman running over a drawbridge and into a fortress, disappearing under the ramparts moving from left to right. The next shot could have the camera inside the walls and at a lower angle as he passes through the gate and across the screen. It is important to realize that this second shot should also have the character moving from the left side of the screen to the right.

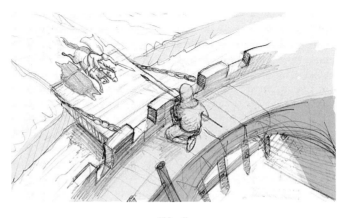

"Yes"

"Yes"

"No"

As we all know, there are exceptions to all rules and times when other factors govern one's choices but usually the orientation of even stationary objects in a shot should remain consistent with other adjoining shots. There is nothing to be gained by confusing the audience or breaking the 180-degree rule when the purpose is to tell your story clearly.

Continuity of Content

Continuity of content is a general expression of the idea of story clarity. It is important for the storyboard artist to remember that the audience does not know the logic of your story until you show them. This sounds simple but problems often arise because we know our own story and we forget that the audience does not know what we know. The audience will be seeing your shots for the first time and then only for a few seconds. If information is not simple and clear, the audience will miss important story points and end up confused for the rest of the film. There are many ways to confuse an audience. Although I cannot discuss every possibility in this chapter, I would like to point out a couple of common storyboard shortcomings.

Disjointed Shots

Scenes depicting bad drug trips and nightmares, earthquakes, pillaging barbarians, and general chaos may show extremely different shots together to instill in the audience a sense of what it feels like to be disoriented. However, the rest of the time you need to provide an uncomplicated flow of visual information to the viewer. Continuity of content requires that you show us all the "pieces" we need to see, usually in a natural, chronological order. It is important that you do not make the viewer work too hard in order to know what is going on. It is your story that should engage the audience. Make the story easy to understand. Storyboards help you to establish both visual continuity and continuity of content. However, since storyboard artists are inherently "too close" to the storyboards to see them objectively, show your boards to others who do not know the story you are working on to see if it makes sense to them. Ultimately, the success of your film will not only depend on whether you understand and like what you see, but rather on whether you have communicated well to others.

Visual continuity also requires the story artist to build an appropriate evolution of shape, color, space, lighting, and other formal elements of design as the story develops. The visual design elements can either harmonize or contrast from one shot to the next. Harmonious or similar shapes and colors suggest small changes in the story. Contrasts, big changes in the design or composition, usually suggest more extreme shifts in content, emotion, or action. Filmmakers often will show a film for several minutes with fairly constant, harmoniously designed images until the moment when something that will change the story happens, like when the villain appears. When the villain appears his color may be different, the shapes and tones in the background could go from horizontal to diagonal, the camera angle may be very low for the first time in the film, and the lighting might be harsh with strong shadows after having been soft and even in earlier shots. It is important to avoid making strong changes in the design from one shot to the next if the story does not have a strong thematic or emotional shift on that shot.

Too Big of a Gap

Story clarity and continuity can fall apart if there is not enough information. Let's say a character is walking down the street and then the scene cuts to that character inside a house sitting in a chair.

This could work if the audience believes that time has passed and we are now in some new place. However, if you want us to know that the character went into a particular house that belongs to someone he knows who the character discovers is not at home . . . , you will have to explain these things. The character may need to be seen walking up to and perhaps into the house, searching for the other character, looking into several rooms and then sitting down in the chair. As this character is looking for someone you may need to show him walking through a bedroom door and then cut to a reverse shot showing the character's face looking around inquisitively. Then you may need to show the character's point of view revealing what he sees and does not see as he looks. After that it may be necessary to show the character's face again so the audience knows that the character is surprised or confused and has recognized that no one is there. Then you may need to show him walk over to the chair and sit down. Keep reminding yourself that the audience does not know what's going on in your story or in the character's mind until you show them.

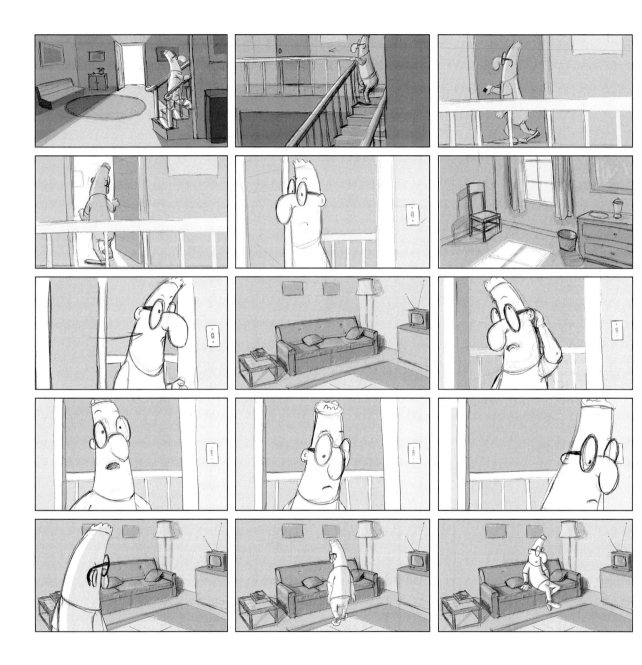

Shot types:

Establishing Shot, Reverse Shot, Cut on the Look, POV, and Reaction Shot

Establishing Shot

The opening shot in a scene can be used to show the viewer where the story will be taking place: in the woods, in a castle, at the circus, or in this case in a middle-class suburb. This is often a long shot that gives a lot of general information about the location or event, the time of day, and weather conditions. The establishing shot can also give us a feeling for the story. It could show bright houses with trimmed hedges and a bicycle on the lawn or there could be a dark, ramshackle mansion with an iron gate and dead trees. The feeling of peacefulness or peril could be suggested through the shapes, patterns, and lighting. The visual style of the film can be revealed. All of these things set a visual context for all other relationships in the scene, making the establishing shot very important.

Reverse Shot and Over the Shoulder

A reverse shot points the camera back in the opposite direction from a previous shot. If we watch our character walk through a doorway and we are looking at his back, the next shot may show a camera view from inside the room he's just entered from a front view. This is often used if two characters are facing each other having a conversation. The camera will show a "front on" shot of one character talking and then reverse the camera and show the other person listening or responding. This kind of shot may also be done "over the shoulder." As the name implies, the camera is behind the character. The character's shoulder and/or part of her head can be seen in the foreground as the audience sees what the character is facing or looking at. Many filmed conversations will use a combination of these shots. Sometimes students confuse these camera reversals with violating the 180-degree rule but that is different. The 180-degree rule requires that you keep your subjects oriented to either the right or left side of the screen but it does not prohibit you from reversing the position of the camera. However, even when reverse shots are used, as in a conversation, it is often advisable to shift one character more to the left side of the screen instead of in the center and the other person more to the right and to keep these relative positions consistent throughout the conversation. It is also important to keep the camera angled up or down if one character is higher or lower than the other.

Cut on the Look and Point of View (POV)

When a filmmaker shows the character looking at something and then shows the audience what the character has seen just as if we are seeing it through the character's eyes, this is called a *point of view* or *POV* shot. So, if a character is looking up at the second floor bedroom window of a house, the next shot will show the window as that character sees it from that low angle and at that distance. If the character then looks down at his watch, the camera may show the character looking at his wrist and then cut to show a down angle shot of the arm and the wristwatch. It is important when your character sees something to show the audience first, that he is looking at something or in some direction and then what he sees. If the audience does not see what the character has seen it will not know what the character has experienced. If the audience does not know what the character has experienced, the plot and the audience's identification with the character's emotions may be lost. The storyboard artist may also want to show us how the character reacts to what he has seen, so that we understand what the character is thinking and feeling.

Thinking, Deciding, Reaction Shots

While the animator or actor is responsible for the final version of the character's performance the storyboard artist initiates it by drawing the iconic poses and facial expressions that are appropriate for this point in the story. As Barry Cook, Animator, Story Artist, and Director of Disney's *Mulan*, put it, "I would not advise leaving the acting to the animators for a simple reason: if it is not clear in boards what your characters are feeling, the scene will never get to the animators." If a storyboard were to show a character looking into an empty room, the following shot could be the character's POV (point of view) of the empty room. Then the next shot showing a close-up of the character's face

looking confused and thinking, "Why is there no one here?" This is the reaction shot. Reaction shots are often overlooked by beginners. Beginning story artists often only show *what* is happening, the action, and leave out showing the character's response to what is happening, the acting. Without the acting you do not have a dramatic story. You only have a description, a report. Drama requires emotion.

We need to know what the character thinks and feels about what she has experienced. The storyboard artist does this by showing the audience the reaction shot. These reactions reveal our character's attitude, personality, and motivations, her internal dialogue and understanding of the situation. Reaction shots are indispensable to good storytelling.

Although this image may be a bit corny, it would be preferable to having no representation of your character's mood or state of mind.

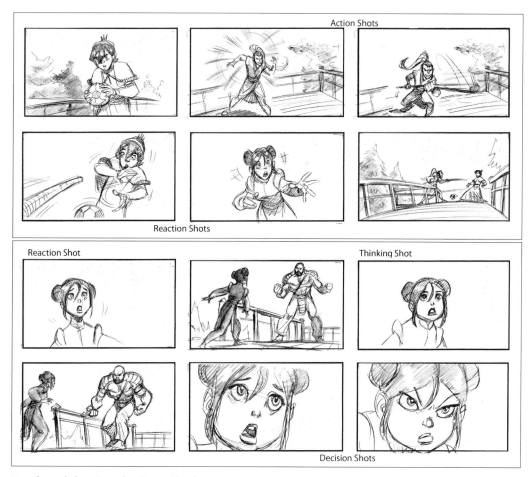

Storyboard drawings by Steve Gordon

Insert, Cutaway, Cut on the Action, Cross Cutting

In the early days of film, filmmakers often had a camera running continuously from a single location as the action moved in front of the lens much the way we would see a play being performed on a stage. With experience and artistic vision, filmmakers soon realized that the possibilities of cinematography offered many more exciting choices. Complex angles, multiple views, and simultaneous actions could be shown in a way that the audience could follow when the shots were edited together effectively.

Insert

An insert shot is cut into the flow of an action and is usually designed to show the audience some specific piece of information, often in a close-up, sometimes a still image.

If a character looks at his watch you may see an insert that shows a close-up of the watch so the audience knows it is 5 minutes until midnight. An insert could also be something that the director wants the audience to see but the main character is unaware of. In live action, these shots are usually added, or inserted, during the editing process.

Cutaway

Cutaway refers to shots that show images that are not in the main action but are usually happening at the same time. If a knight is fighting a dragon you may see the camera "cut away" to the damsel in distress as she shields her eyes when her hero appears to be faltering in the battle. In a cutaway you can show the actions and reactions of these other participants without stopping the main action. The knight and dragon could be fighting near the edge of a rocky cliff and a cutaway may show small rocks that have been kicked loose during the battle rolling off the edge of the cliff and falling down into an abyss. Sometimes a cutaway is used to reveal the environment to create atmosphere and a sense of what a place is like and feels like. During the knight and dragon battle, a cutaway shot may show a pile of human bones and armor telling us that many other knights have tried and failed to defeat the dragon.

Cut on the Action

If an outlaw is going to be hanged in a Western town, a distant shot may show the outlaw's body start to drop through the trap door. A cutaway may show a close-up of the rope pull straight and tight where it is attached at the top of the gallows. Then the camera may return to the distant shot of the outlaw dangling at the end of the rope. This cutting away from the main action to show a detail is sometimes called *cut on the action*. It suggests to the audience that the main action is continuing while the detail was being shown. This same "cut on the action" could happen the opposite way, starting with a detail shot, cutting away to a distant shot, and then returning to the original close-up.

Cross Cutting

Another editing device which is similar to the cutaway is cross cutting. Cross cutting is used to show two actions that are happening at the same time. This becomes particularly important if the two actions or events are going to come together and create one major action. In the storyboard segment of the pirate rabbit by student Maria Clapsis (fig. 60 and 61), a lizard captain is above deck and a pirate rabbit is below deck entering a doorway leaving a gun powder trail on the floor. Later, the rabbit has an encounter with a hanging skeleton that causes him to get frightened and drop his cigar. In the storyboards shown, cross cutting allows the audience to see that the cigar has started a fire that keeps growing next to the gunpowder. At the same time the pirates, oblivious to the fire, are preparing to shoot a canon ball at a passing ship. In the end, the cigar fire near the gunpowder and the attempt to shoot the cannon simultaneously reach a climax and the pirate ship blows up. The passing ship is unharmed but the pirate ship is sunk.

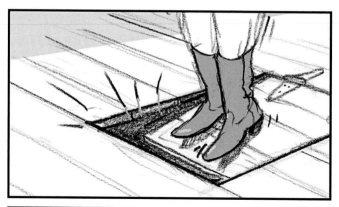

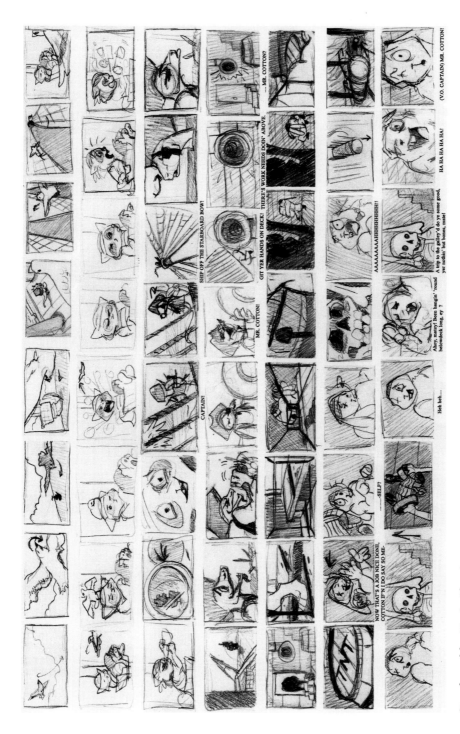

Storyboard by Maria Clapsis

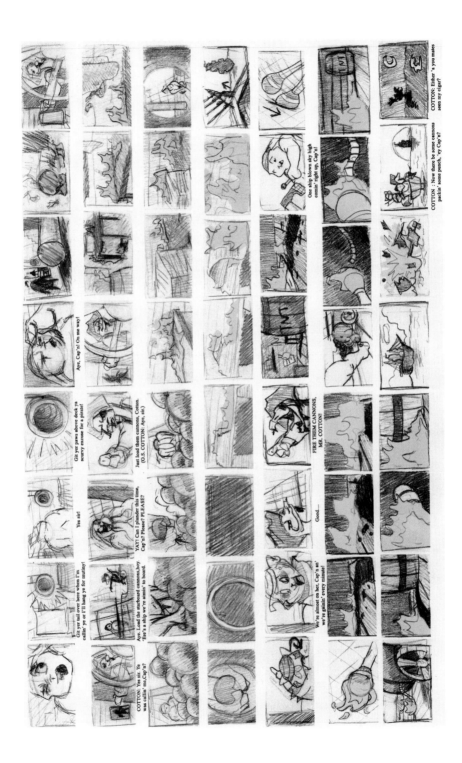

Split Screen, Collage, and Superimposition

In order to clarify simultaneous events or images, filmmakers have tried a number of ways to show two or more pictures on the screen at the same time. These devices can be very effective if used correctly. The problem is that they tend to draw a lot of attention to themselves and may seem artificial or contrived. A split screen is often used when two characters are talking on the phone. The two shots of the two characters are simply shown, each in his or her own location, on a divided screen.

Split screen

A similar effect is sometimes created when we see a side view of a character outside of a door and another character on the other side of the door or wall. The cross-section of the wall serves as a natural device to split the screen. A collage technique may show two or more images on the screen together or in quick succession, perhaps with cross dissolves as in a montage. Superimposition, another technique, usually refers to a semitransparent image overlying a primary image. Superimposition is often used to show a memory. A picture-in-picture may have a new rectangle appear on the screen revealing a second image. There are a myriad of variations and rare types of shots used in films that I will not cover in this chapter. Books such as *Setting Up Your Shots* by Jeremy Vineyard and *From Word to Image* by Marcie Begleiter cover types of shots and terminology in greater depth.

Transitions

Beyond the types of shots, storyboarding also involves transitions between cuts. When I refer to transitions, I am speaking of two kinds. One kind is technical and refers to the mechanical process of film or digital editing, the resulting visual effect, and its meaning for the viewer. The other kind is pictorial and refers to the types of pictures you are putting next to one another and how they move the ideas along. These transitions can expand time, compress time, and enhance the mood and energy of a sequence. Although this is more apparent in the animatic or final editing stage, the planning and anticipation of transitions are part of the blueprint of any film. As Nathan Greno, Disney Story Artist and Story Supervisor for

Disney's upcoming feature, *Bolt*, put it, "I try to keep editing transitions in mind if they help to tell the story I am boarding—otherwise I let the editor worry about the editing. The more you can do up front, the better it will help everyone else." If your are making your own film, you may be the story artist and the final editor. So it is a good idea to start planning how you will use transitions to help tell your story.

Technical Editing Transitions

Every change from one shot to the next is called a cut. If the filmmaker decides to put some black frames or white frames between shots or fade one shot out as the other simultaneously fades in, the shots will read differently. Common technical transitions are the standard cut, the cut or fade to black or to white, and the cross dissolve. There are many others like the iris (see Fig. B73-B76) that are used for special reasons, which I will not go into in this chapter. A fade to black can suggest that time has passed between the end of one shot and the beginning of the next. This can happen quickly or very slowly and the effect is a sense of duration. A cross dissolve will show one shot becoming progressively transparent and fading away as it is simultaneously replaced by the next shot fading in. Such transitions may suggest we are in another place perhaps at another time. Variables such as the type of image, duration of transitions, and the story context will have an effect on the way that our audience reacts to our film transitions. However, these transitions will dramatically affect your story so you must often consider your story and the technical transitions in tandem. You can choose to draw these transitions or it may be enough to simply write, fade, or cross dissolve on your storyboards. If you produce an animatic, you can show the transitions between your story panels and reveal the effect more completely.

Cross Dissolve

Fade to Black

Fade to White

Iris in

Pictorial Transitions and Match Cuts

Unlike a single painting or sculpture, most narrative film is made of a continuous series of changing images. One can put very different images next to each other or very similar images next to each other. When one cuts to an image that is noticeably similar to the previous image, it is called a *match cut*. If a character is eating and begins to move a spoon toward his mouth and then the camera cuts to a close-up of him completing the action and putting the spoon in his mouth, this is a match cut even if the camera has moved. The two shots are tied visually and thematically together by the action.

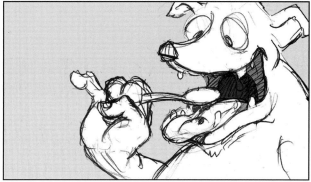

Match Cut

Match cuts like this can be used to create a natural flow of images so the cuts are barely noticed. Match cuts can also be used to relate two different kinds of images. A pair of shots could cut from an image of the round glowing sun to an image of a round glowing light bulb in a room at night. This will not only create a comfortable transition between two similar looking objects but it may communicate to the viewer that the passage of time has caused the daylight of the sun to be replaced by the nighttime light of the electric bulb. In this case, the two images are matched by content, shape and perhaps even color.

Match Cut

One could also match images by movement such as a car racing down a road transitioning to a train going down a railroad track. A match cut of a female scientist holding up a test tube in a laboratory dissolving to the same woman holding up a baby bottle just before she feeds her baby could tell the story of a woman giving up her career to be a stay-at-home mother. Match cuts like these are a way of slicing through time and complex details to force relationships between images and ideas. They can often allow us to move through a great deal of story time in a very small amount of movie time. They can often make changes that would otherwise seem harsh or discordant seem more visually agreeable and harmonious.

Clean Entrance/Exit

A clean entrance happens when you show a place and then without a camera cut you see a character or a car or a dog enter the scene. The clean exit will show a character leave a scene and the shot will remain on the place he has departed from for a bit before the camera cuts to the next shot. To show the location before the character arrives or after the character departs changes the viewer's reading of the passage of time. If you see a girl riding away on a bicycle and the camera cuts before the bike leaves the frame and the next shot is another view of the girl on the bike, the audience can usually assume that the cuts are instantaneous, that no time has elapsed between the two shots.

If the character rides completely off the screen and the camera shows the empty school yard she was previously riding by and then cuts to a shot of the girl's house and the bicyclist comes riding into the screen, the audience may assume that some time had passed between the time she rode by the school yard and the time she arrived at her house.

We will be convinced that these scenes are not taking place in the uninterrupted time of the film, but represent the beginning and end of a journey from which the middle has been extracted, perhaps for the sake of expediency or to more quickly get to the important parts of the story. Showing the girl spend 20 minutes riding from the school yard to her house might be very boring and insignificant to the story. You should not let your story get bogged down with inconsequential information. However, other times the story may require that you show someone doing something that takes a long, long time.

Jump Cut

The boredom or weariness of a long drawn out action may be a central point in the story. Rather than show the camera on someone as she is in the act of waiting all night you may show jump cuts. Technically, a jump cut is simply a cut where the same character or image moves abruptly from one shot to the next, sometimes breaking the flow of time and space. If a person is waiting, there may be a shot of him sitting in a chair. Then the camera cuts to the character slouched back in the chair. A third cut may have him bent over with his elbows on his knees or up walking around in the room. This would create the feeling that we are seeing short excerpts from a long, boring period of time. Jump cuts could be used to speed up the portrayal of the duration of time while the audience still understands that this represents a long wait.

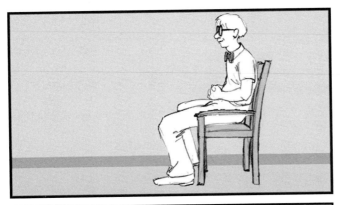

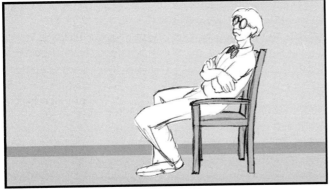

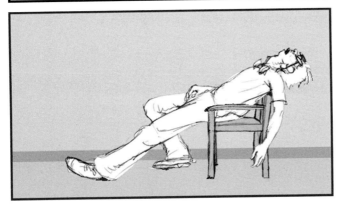

Jump cuts to show passage of time

A film that lasts one minute may tell a story that takes place over many years or even centuries. Storytellers can speed up time, slow down time, move forward and backward in time. The passage of time is manipulated to allow the storyteller to move to the important story points and cut through the less significant events. A storyboard artist makes choices about how the story's time and reality will be communicated to achieve the clearest and most effective telling of the story.

Visualizing Time and Movement

Another aspect of revealing the passage of time is the representation of movement. From the earliest cave paintings to the most recent animated film, artists have been trying to create still images that embody an expression of movement. This is because most living things move and embodying movement will bring the artist closer to embodying life. And all great art embodies a sense of life. The history of art is filled with images of flying angels and battling soldiers on running horses. Some modern artists such as the Futurists and Cubists created abstracted representations showing multiple aspects of humans and objects suggesting the images were moving or that the viewer was moving around the objects. When filmmaking came into existence many secrets were revealed about the nature of movement. One of the earliest and still the greatest documentations of the movement of people and animals was conducted by Eadweard Muybridge. In 1877, his technique of creating a series of still images of a horse trotting proved that all four of a horse's hooves were off the ground at points during the action. The experiments by scientists such as Harold Edgarton in the mid-20th century using special lighting devices and high-speed cameras were able to capture shots of a bullet passing through an apple with the clear image of the bullet suspended in air. Some of the photos Edgarton made had shutter speeds of one one-hundred-millionth of a second. So the questions are "What can we learn from this, what do things look like when they move, and how do we capture this impression of movement in a still image?"

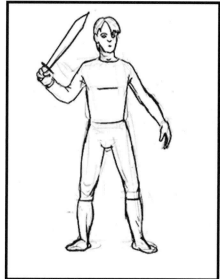

No Movement

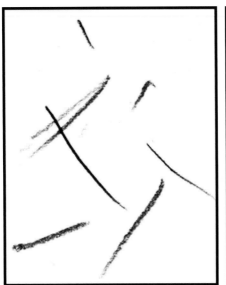 

Movement

Storyboard by Steve Gordon

Graphic Representation of Movement

There are devices of graphic representation that can suggest movement or restrict movement. Buildings are designed to not move. They are typically made of straight lines based on horizontals and verticals like a soldier standing at attention. Therefore, horizontals and verticals may restrict movement. Movement is suggested by diagonals and curves. Humans and animals tilt and turn and bend. We move through space in paths that define arcs and can spin, creating serpentine patterns. Drawings of moving things require the application of these elements. A running character may have her feet completely off the ground like Muybridge's horse. She may be leaning forward with her hair and clothing flapping in the wind behind her. Speed lines and multiple images can be used to create a sort of "comet's tail" effect following an object. Storyboard drawings need to look alive. They need to move and act and feel in order to overcome their static reality and to communicate the heightened action that animation requires.

Principles of Movement

Anticipation, Squash and Stretch, Arcs, Follow Through and Overlapping Action

Animators have discovered over the years that certain predictable principles can be applied to animated characters and other moving forms. These help to bridge that gap between the time-based dynamics of real-world physics and static reality of the drawn or virtual image. The following 5 of "the 12 principles of animation" pertain particularly to movement.

Anticipation

Before a character can jump off a box he must anticipate. That means he must contract his muscles, squat down, bend his knees, and maybe bring his arms and elbows up behind him. He may even scrunch up his facial features. Anticipation is the way the character builds up the energy to jump. Through this action, he will also be communicating to the audience that he is preparing to jump. Anticipation is both psychological and physical. One usually anticipates in the opposite direction of the main action.

Squash and Stretch

The principle of squash and stretch is an exaggerated sense of elasticity applied to show how things distort when they move and when they stop. When a character jumps off a box, she will stretch as she falls through the air and squash as her legs absorb the weight of the body collapsing onto itself. Even the head of a hammer may squash when it strikes a board. Though it may not be necessary to apply extreme exaggeration on each movement you depict, the effects of squash and stretch in your storyboard drawings may have to be overstated to communicate the force and energy of the movement.

Arcs

Mechanical things such as cars and rockets are distinguished by the fact that they appear to travel in a straight path. However, when most things, especially organic forms, move through space they move in arcs. When a character swings his arm or lifts his head or jumps off a box, the path of action will most always be an arc. If you are showing speed lines, they should reflect the curved movement.

Follow Through and Overlapping Action

Follow through suggests that something will keep moving in the direction of its force until some resistance causes it to stop. When a baseball player hits a ball his bat keeps swinging around in its arc until it stops behind his head. If a rider's horse stops suddenly the rider may go flying over the top of the horse. This is closely related to overlapping action, which suggests that different parts of the main body of a character or an object will move or stop at different times. If a character jumps off a box his coattail may not come down until after his feet have hit and perhaps not until he is starting to stand upright. Follow through explains that a form keeps moving in its designated path until something stops it, like friction or hitting another object. Overlapping action describes the way these different parts may move at different times. So if you draw a character landing from a jump, his knees may be bending from the squash but his coattail may still be up in the air.

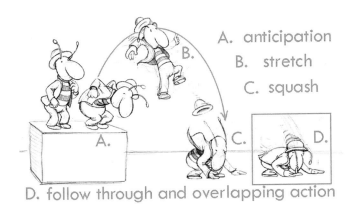

A. anticipation
B. stretch
C. squash
D. follow through and overlapping action

Multiple Images

If a character needs to move through a scene in a particular way, the storyboard artist can either show several panels that represent different stages of the action or one shot that shows multiple, staggered images to describe different positions. The choice is determined by the need for clarity. The goal should be to have one idea in each board so there may need to be many panels to show a shot from a single camera position if, for instance, a squirrel was walking across the counter in a candy store continually searching for goodies. The squirrel may be lifting this and looking under that as he makes his way across the counter. One should probably do a drawing for each action, for each idea.

If, on the other hand, the squirrel is simply walking across the counter, the boards may want only to show the path he takes. In this case a beginning and end drawing with arrows connecting them in one storyboard panel may suffice. Arrows pointing left and right, up, down, forward, backward, and following arcs can "stand in" for movements in the still images of a storyboard and can be very helpful to the direction and clarity of actions.

Camera Moves

Camera operators can hold a camera in their hand, put it on a car or an airplane, or push it around on a dolly. Cranes and trucks that ride on tracks have been used to move the audience's vantage point to wherever the filmmaker wants it to be. Digital technology allows cameras to follow bullets into the bodies of victims, be plunged into molten lava, and see through the eyes of an erratically moving dragonfly. Advancements in lenses and internal camera technology also create many options. A storyboard artist should know when and what kind of camera moves to use.

Trucks and Zooms

Trucks and zooms will produce similar results, but they are not the same. A zoom on a face in a crowd of characters will cause the size of the face to be "blown up" on the screen along with everything else in the frame. In the truck, the rest of the crowd will not grow but the foreground people will be seen passing by as the camera moves toward the face. A truck on that character's face will be closer to the experience of walking through the crowd until you are physically close to her and her face is close to you. This is because the zoom is done with the camera lens and magnifies the light coming through, whereas the truck actually moves the camera through the crowd toward the main character. This difference will make a difference in the way you are allowing the audience to experience the action. This physical difference evokes a different emotional response and represents a significantly different way of telling your story.

Zoom

Truck

Representing Camera Moves: Pans, Tracks, Zooms, and Extended Frames

If you have decided that it is necessary to show the camera moving as part of your story idea, there are some standard ways to represent this in the storyboard. If a dog sees something good to eat like a pie but the baker is standing guard, the camera may choose to show the character's POV as he looks at the pie and then at his obstacle, the baker. Instead of a cut, you may want the camera to swing or rotate from one view to the other. This type of shot needs to be shown by indicating the movement of the camera. The storyboard artist can draw framing boxes around each of the views, focusing on one and then the other view with arrows or lines that connect the two boxes.

This technique can be used for a zoom shot as well. The panel would show the whole scene with framing boxes corresponding to the film's aspect ratio used to show close-up and over-view areas with lines or arrows connecting them.

Sometimes the camera moves cover such a great distance that they cannot be contained within one standard-sized frame. If the camera follows beside a cat as it walks across a floor and jumps onto a windowsill, this is referred to as a tracking shot. It may be necessary to show the distance covered as a storyboard panel that is wider or higher than normal. The character can be shown at two or more positions along the way. A framing box would be shown around several character positions to explain how the camera is framing the character at different points during the action. Once again, these framing boxes can be connected by arrows or lines.

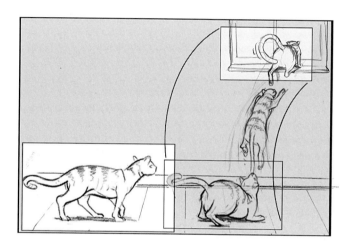

Sometimes zooms and pans or zooms and dollys, called *zollys*, happen at the same time. If camera moves are important to telling your story, then you are responsible for showing them. You may choose to show it with framing boxes and arrows or as a series of individual drawings on different panels. You must be clear about what you are trying to show so the storyboards depict how the film version of your story is going to read.

Camera Placement

Where you put the camera is where you are visually and emotionally putting the audience. You can either keep them at a distance watching the action or make them see and feel like they are in the midst of the events like participants. There is a right time and a wrong time for both of these approaches. It is essential to how you tell a story and a decision you must make on nearly every board. Beginner story artists often do not exploit their options in camera placement. As story artist and teacher, Jim Story said, "One of the most prominent stumbling blocks in student boards is a tendency to 'lock down' the camera and to view everything at the same size as if it were on stage."

Many boxing movies show the actor swinging punches directly at the camera or waking up from the floor with an up angle of the ceiling lights and the referee counting to 10. This can make us feel as though the experience is happening to us.

Other times we are in the audience looking over the tops of other people's heads. Sometimes the camera takes us completely out of the action and we are looking down from above like a scientist might look at specimens through a microscope. The purpose is not to be fancy with the camera for its own sake. Too many unnecessary camera moves are surely as problematic as locking the camera down. Your story's appropriate feelings of mystery, intimacy, or indifference can be induced by carefully choosing your audience's vantage point through good camera placement.

How Much Information

Students often ask how many panels will I need and how finished should they be? The answer depends on your story and how you are telling it. A filmmaker can show a character going through a door with one shot or ten shots if the situation calls for it. Each board should represent one idea. The camera may cut back and forth between the inside and outside if, for instance, someone is inside watching the door open. If the character hesitates or struggles with the door the boards may be quite involved. If value and light are critical to the telling of your story or something's color is an important element, then you may need to show that in your boards. Otherwise, simple line drawings may do the job. If a character comes walking out of the fog, then you need to show the fog in the environment where the shots take place. Other times atmosphere and weather conditions may not be a concern.

Clarity

Nearly every storyboard artist, director, and producer I've interviewed mentioned the need to be clear in your storyboards. We cannot go back and re-tell the story in our short film; it has to work the first time. Shots need to be unambiguous and so should your storyboards. Find a simple, clear drawing style. Avoid unnecessary details. Too much detail can actually make the idea harder to read but be complete with the ideas you are portraying. Be bold. Faint graphite pencil drawings that are too weak to see will not work. Use a felt tip or china

marker or at least a soft, broad-tipped pencil. More and more often, artists are scanning their drawings into Photoshop or some similar program to enhance the clarity. Contrast can be boosted, tones can be added, cropping and re-framing are easy, and layers can allow you to use the same character or background drawing over several times and keep them consistent without re-drawing.

Boarding Dialogue, Acting

It is often said that dialogue should be like background music. You should be able to turn the sound off and still know what is happening in the story. This is mostly true and it suggests, as I have been saying, that it is the visual information, a character's gesture, facial expressions, and environment, that do the communicating. Imagine a wife is waiting for her philandering husband, who is three hours late for supper. She may say, "Oh, I'm so glad you decided to join us." Of course what she really means is, "You thoughtless jerk, you don't care how much inconvenience you cause me." The words are only part of the story and sometimes a fairly insignificant part. Your storyboard panels need to show us that a character's body language communicates his true mood or state of mind as the words are being spoken. Animation tends to use exaggerated body gestures and facial expressions. Make a video of yourself or another actor delivering the lines or get a mirror and try to find the primary facial expressions you need and then caricature them. In animation all the acting is created on paper, in the computer, or with clay, and so forth. As Frank Gladstone, producer and animation artist, said, "This is one of the reasons many board artists were animators first. Like animators, storyboard folks have to understand acting . . . and how acting choices help to establish both narrative context and subtext. Of course, like actors and animators, board artists should develop good and consistent observation skills." Observation skills mean paying attention to real life and how people behave. Watch how a parent scolds a child. Watch two children negotiate over a toy. Watch someone talking on a phone. Become a student of acting, of human behavior.

What?

Forgot What?

Oh!!!

Uh, he he. . . .

Pitching

Pitching is the process where storyboard artists show and explain the boards to others. During the pitch, the storyboard artist will point to individual panels and tell us what is going on, often making sound effects or speaking in the different voices of the characters with the appropriate expression. The pitch will indicate the pace of events by going through the boards faster or slower. It requires that one is not shy and perhaps even has a bit of acting ability. The pitch is presented to inform other members of a story team or the director and clients. A pitch can help "sell" the storyboards and get them approved for animation, not because they have been made to seem more entertaining than they actually are but because they have been brought to life a bit more. In story teams, such as the major studios have, you can expect that your pitch will result in your story being changed, rearranged, and even thrown out sometimes. As Nathan Greno, Supervising Story Artist, Walt Disney Feature Animation put it, "A successful storyboard artist is one that is open to new ideas. You CAN'T fall in love with your boards. Your boards are not the final film—they won't be on the screen. Don't spend too much time on your boards—they will most likely be completely thrown out at some point. If that sounds too depressing, you best find another department to work in. Story is subjective. Your director is going to ask for changes. To be a great story artist; you will have to be open-minded to throwing your work away. Even if you completely disagree with your director, you are going to have to make the changes. It doesn't matter if you think the director is crazy." Stories can be told many different ways. Be willing to change your plan often while searching for the best solutions.

Pacing

Pacing defines the rate of the action and the cuts. A dry, flat story presentation may have the cuts at even intervals. A stronger presentation may linger lazily on some images and present others in rapid-fire succession. The number of film cuts may increase as the tension and action build. The audience will feel a sense of urgency even if it is not aware that the cuts are coming quicker. The best way to know if the pacing is working is to see the images change during the pitch or to make the boards into an animatic or progression reel. However, from the very beginning you must anticipate the pacing of your film and imagine the timing of the cuts.

Progression/Story Reels

In large studios, the animators will see what is called a *story* or *progression reel* at several points during the production of the film. The first version would be made almost entirely of the storyboard drawings with a scratch track, a substitute dialogue and/or sound effects track. This is how the hundreds of people working on the film can be kept informed about the kind of film they are making. As the project progresses, artists see updated versions of the reel. The next version may have some of the storyboards replaced by anima-tion. Perhaps a few color scenes would be cut in. Maybe some of the actor's recorded dialogue would be inserted to replace the scratch track and some of the final music score may be heard.

Animatics

Digital technology has provided nearly every story artist with a number of computer programs that allow them to make a progression reel from their storyboards. This digital video version of a storyboard is usually called an animatic. You can photograph or scan the drawings and play them back with the correct timing and many of the editing transitions that will be used in the final film. Sound can be added as well as text and even some camera moves and simulated effects. This is very useful for the independent filmmaker. The process brings you that much closer to the full realization of how the film is going to play before you make the final version. During the animatic stage, it is easier to see if transitions are working and if rhythm and pacing feel correct for the story. You can coordinate the soundtrack with the images and generally have a clearer vision of the film. How far you go with the animatic varies. Some of the animatics on the DVD that comes with this book show a basic skeleton of the shots, while others are nearly films in their own right.

Digital Storyboards

Some video game studios are doing all their storyboards and story presentations digitally. Feature animation studios are beginning to change as well. As Paul Briggs, a relatively new member of the Walt Disney Feature Animation story team, said, "I personally start out by thumbnailing on paper and figuring out the major beats in the sequence. I'll then work all digital on a 21" Cintiq monitor drawing all my boards in Photoshop. I usually work straight ahead but once I'm done with the sequence, I'm always going back into it and reworking it. Whatever you feel comfortable using and best conveys your ideas is what's important though. A lot of artists still draw on paper and use chalk, crayon, marker, pens, etc. Others work all digital using Photoshop or Painter." Paul Briggs also said that he presents his work to the directors by projecting the drawings using a computer program which allows him to move and delete boards as well as change dialogue. This will surely become more prevalent in the future, so it is a good idea to become familiar with these programs and the digital drawing tablet.

Summary

- Storyboards plan and communicate the shots and transitions of a film.
- Drawing skill and versatility are essential to professional storyboard artists.
- A knowledge of film language and cinematography is essential.
- Design elements embody the emotional messages in a film.
- Thumbnailing is how we start the visual process.

- Work to achieve continuity of direction, content, and design.
- There are a number of standard shots and transitions that are used most often.
- Manipulate the passage of time with the right cuts and transitions.
- Storyboards can represent both the movement of objects and the camera.
- Camera placement can help determine the audience's emotional attachment.
- Boarding dialogue involves special issues.
- Pitching is how storyboards are often presented to others.
- Animatics reveal the pacing and transitions as a filmed version of the boards.
- The storyboarding process is becoming progressively more digital.

Recommended Readings

1. Don Bluth, *Don Bluth's Art of Storyboard*

2. John Canemaker, *Paper Dreams*

3. Wayne Gilbert, *Simplified Drawing for Planning Animation*

4. Will Eisner, *Comics and Sequential Art*

5. Frank Thomas and Ollie Johnston, *The Illusion of Life*

Storyboarding: An Interview with Nathan Greno, Walt Disney Feature Animation

Nathan Greno attended Columbus College of Art and Design and later completed a Disney Animation Internship in Orlando, Florida. Nathan began working full-time as a cleanup artist in the Disney traditional animation studio in 1996 and then in the Disney story department in 1998. He is now a Story Supervisor at Walt Disney Feature Animation, currently heading up story development on the upcoming feature, *Bolt*, slated for release in 2008.

Q: What background skills do storyboard artists need to be successful? What would you tell a student?

Nathan: To be a successful storyboard artist, you need an overworking brain and plenty of imagination. You need to be able to express your thoughts visually. You need to understand acting, staging, mood, and lighting. You must be able to write dialog and create characters. A storyboard artist creates the blueprint for the film. Storyboarding is the foundation of a film. With practice and training you will get better but it is a skill that can't be learned.

Q: How can one become a better storyboard artist?

Nathan: You get better at drawing by PRACTICE! Board your own ideas and pitch them to friends. Find a script of a movie you haven't seen and draw a sequence from it—then watch the movie and see what choices the filmmakers made. You will get better—and your drawing skills will quickly improve. Draw different kinds of sequences. If you feel you are better at action, board a sequence with subtle acting and dialog. If you are better at subtle acting, board a chase sequence. Challenge yourself.

One thing to avoid is "stock" expressions. Unless your project calls for it, stay away from 1930s hammy acting. Act out your sequence before you draw it. Have a mirror sitting on your drawing table. Natural expressions are an amazing tool to have in your belt. The trick to drawing natural expressions: Less is usually more.

Q: Are there special characteristics that you find professional story artists have in common? What makes the successful ones successful?

Nathan: A successful storyboard artist is one that is open to ideas. You *can't* fall in love with your boards. Be willing to change. Your boards are not the final film. Don't spend too much time on your boards—they will likely be thrown out at some point. If that sounds too depressing, you best find another discipline to work in. Story is subjective. Your director is going to ask for changes. To be a great story artist, you will have to be ready to throw your work away. Even if you disagree and you think the director is crazy. At the end of the day, you must respect your position. It's your job to make the project as great as it can be. But it's not "your" project.

Q: Have you looked at any student storyboards? What do you think is most often lacking in them?

Nathan: Recently we had a student portfolio review. Many had a similar problem: it was hard to follow their boards. Many students don't like to draw backgrounds. They don't set their characters in an understandable environment. You should be able to follow boards without reading the dialog. Try this: watch a movie with the sound off. Usually you will still be able to tell what is going on because of the environment, staging, and lighting—and expressions! Your boards should work this way. At a portfolio review there will not be enough time to look through every single panel of your boards and read every single line of your dialog. Within a dozen drawings a reviewer should be able to know what is going on in your boards.

There's a series of graphic novels that I can't recommend enough: *Bone* by Jeff Smith. They have started coloring them—but they were originally printed in black and white. Buy the black and white editions. It's amazing how much mood Smith can get without the use of color or grey tones. His acting is incredible—learn from what he's doing.

Q: Can you describe your process?

Nathan: There is no "right way" to storyboard a sequence. I always start with thumbnails. Sometimes I "straight ahead" my sequences and sometimes I board a bunch of key shots (that usually helps me with a big action sequence). What works best for you is the way to go.

Q: What do you find are the main obstacles you have to overcome when you are storyboarding a scene?

Nathan: A good thing to keep in mind is one new idea/action per drawing. Don't have too much going on in one panel or you'll confuse people. Clear simple drawings are a good thing.

Q: How would you describe the difference between storyboarding for film and other kinds of sequential artwork like comic books or book illustration?

Nathan: Comic books and storyboards are cousins—not brothers. I have learned a lot of shorthand drawing tools from comics (rain, simple cityscapes, thunder and lightning, blizzards, underwater or splashing effects, characters or objects moving very fast, outer space sequences, etc.), but comics follow different rules from storyboards. The "camera" jumps around a lot in comics. What works for a comic book story will not work for a storyboarded sequence.

Q: Do you re-draw your panels many times?

Nathan: Don't fall in love with your drawings and don't sweat over them—they need to read clearly, but they are not the final image you will see on the screen. Make sure you are getting your sequences done on time—and make sure they read clearly.

Q: Do you think of yourself as actor, cameraman, editor, designer, and/or all of these things in your job? Have I left anything out?

Nathan: A storyboard artist is an actor, cameraman, editor, and designer—but you also must remember you are a collaborator. You work with others.

Q: How important is presentation? Do you refine your drawings a lot before they are presented to the bosses?

Nathan: That depends on a number of factors. You might throw in a few clean drawings if you've never worked with the director before—you want her to know what a "final" looks like. Rough is usually a good idea if you are exploring a sequence. Tighter, prettier drawings will help sell your sequence—directors like nice drawings. Each case is different—talk to your director to find out what she is looking for. Look at the kind of drawings the other artists are doing on their first passes.

Q: Do you find you have to overstate the action, acting, and so on in order for it to read in the storyboard, or do you leave that problem to be solved by the animator?

Nathan: The more you "leave to the animator" or the layout artist or whoever—the less you'll see "you" in the film. You are making the blueprint of a building—if you don't design the windows, someone else will. You have a deadline so there will only be so much you can accomplish—but the more info you can give, the better the final film will be. People will take your boards and run with them—if the process works correctly, the film will improve with each department. It all starts with the storyboard artist—you are creating the map that everyone else will follow. You better make sure it's a damn good map!

Chapter 8

Staging

Staging in film refers to the way we present an image or an action for our audience. We plan how something is seen and experienced so that the audience gets the story point. You have probably heard people say that something was "staged." This may refer to planning something so it happens a certain way or that something is not a genuine incident, it is artificial. If something happens on stage as in the live theater it is art, it is artificial. Film is also art so it is important for the filmmaker to offer the audience a moving aesthetic experience, while providing the essential storytelling images. It is this marriage of the aesthetic and the narrative that should guide our decisions about staging.

Directing the Eye

Directing the eye refers to using visual devices to get the audience to look where you want them to look in the shot. When an image comes on the screen, the audience may be looking at the lower corner, the center, or the upper third. Perhaps if an object is in the center the audience will look at that. However, if everything is placed in the center all the time it will get monotonous. Sometimes a moving image will draw more attention to itself than a stationary one. A strong color or anything that has greater visual attraction can direct the audience to look at that place on the screen.

Because our images may show for only a short time, we must make sure the audience sees what we need it to see while making the visual experience captivating. We have all seen group-shot photographs where someone would put a circle around or draw an arrow to get us to look at a certain person in the group. A spotlight is used on a live stage to accomplish the same thing. Spotlighting solutions are used in many films as well. In addition to light, graphic shapes, lines, and alignments can similarly lead the viewers' eyes to see what you want them to see.

Place a character in front of the vanishing point in a one-point perspective shot of a room and the receding lines of the vertices toward the vanishing point can direct our eyes to that person, even if there are other people in the room. A case in point is Leonardo Da Vinci's "The Last Supper." Shapes and lines created by foreground objects, shadow patterns, and tone and color patterns can point to the place that you want the audience to see, thereby controlling the viewers' attention.

Storyboard by Maria Clapsis uses leading lines to direct the viewer's eye to the man in the window

Leading lines created by shadows and objects

Spotlight effect to get us to look in the right place

Aspect Ratio, Symmetry, Golden Section, and Rule of Thirds

Aspect ratio is the proportions of your screen. Early television screens were about 1 foot high and 1 foot, 4 inches wide. This is expressed as a 1 : 1.33 aspect ratio. Over the years, the ratio has generally changed to make the screen wider relative to its height. There are a number of reasons for this, one of them being to fill our peripheral vision more completely and approximate the experience of seeing things in real life. All good designs need to relate to the rectangle's proportions and the framing edge.

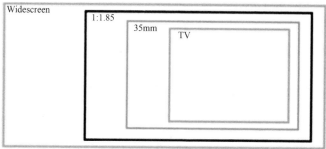

Various Aspect Ratios: most images in this chapter are 1:185

Over the centuries, painters have worked inside of rectangles to build their compositions. The objective has always been to keep the images looking fresh but appropriate to the theme or subject, just like filmmaking. Dynamic images of battles would be designed very differently from portraits. But the search for the best design has led the artist to discover that some relationships seem to work very well and others not so well.

It has already been mentioned that things in the center are boring. Centered things can tend to lack vitality and look inert. It is advisable that you never divide your rectangular frame down the middle either horizontally or vertically unless the purpose is to express division, symmetry, and monotony. The golden section or golden mean is a proportion that would have you divide an 11-inch rectangle at a place that would split it into two shapes, approximately 7 and 4 inches each. This is a ratio of about 1 : 1.618 and is based on a geometric formula that relates the division to the proportion of the whole rectangle. Artists, architects, and other designers had discovered that many things in nature adhere to this proportion so it was considered to be divinely conceived. The golden section is a comfortable, asymmetrical method of organization and is followed by many painters and filmmakers

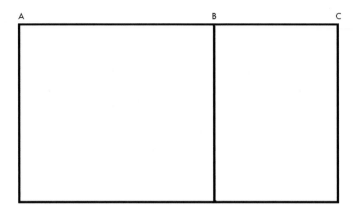

Golden section: *BC* is to *AB* as *AB* is to *AC*

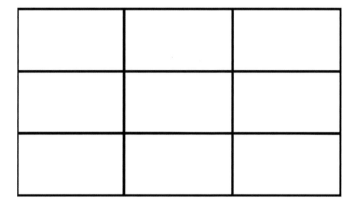

Rule of thirds: the intersections of the horizontal and vertical divisions are hot spots where we should focus the viewer's attention

Many filmmakers are utilizing the rule of thirds for compositional choices. The rule of thirds says that if you divide your screen into thirds vertically and horizontally, the intersection of these lines mark critical locations or "hot spots" on the screen. These hot spots are where the filmmaker should put the important information. This is a comfortable place to focus the audience's attention. If you watch most any well-made films, you'll see the directors using the rule of thirds extensively.

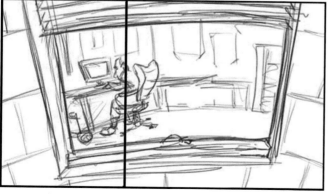

Maria Clapsis, Rule of Thirds

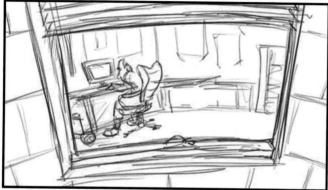

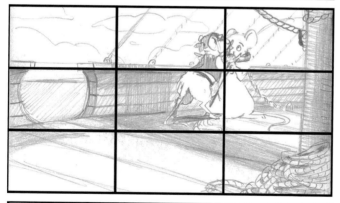

Eric Drobile, Golden Section

Redesigning the Rectangle

In the chapter on storyboarding, we saw how filmmakers can split the screen to show two things happening at two different places at the same time. Montage, superimposition, and picture-in-picture techniques have allowed directors to restructure the film's framing rectangle. Today's relatively widescreen films create special problems for filmmakers as they work to present strong, meaningful visual presentations. It can work to one's advantage to find ways to reshape the area within the larger rectangle to create new and different compositional solutions. We are all familiar with a shot that shows the POV of someone looking through binoculars. This effect is the called "mask shot." It effectively changes the shape of the area of interest. "Frame-in-frame" is a similar compositional device that can allow one to reshape the area of interest and provide focus and variation for the audience. If a camera shoots between the limbs of a tree or into the rearview mirror of a car, the shape of the tree limbs or the edges of the mirror will become a new frame inside the overall shot composition. Sometimes these kinds of shots can make the audience feel like voyeurs looking through gaps in foreground objects as if unseen by the main characters. Other times it can make the audience feel that it is intimate and close up, immersed in an environment where they can reach out and touch the foreground elements. Frame-in-frame shots, like any compositional device, should not be used arbitrarily, but the use of foreground to reshape your area of interest and realign the audience to its experience is an important option.

Frame-in-frame compositions by Maria Clapsis

by Gary Schumer

Redesigning with Tone

Silhouette

We are often trying to create the illusion of a three-dimensional world in our films. Therefore, we sometimes lose sight of the fact that the film is two-dimensional. Films usually happen on a flat screen. A character that in the story has three dimensions is only an illusion of light and actually has only two dimensions. It is only a two-dimensional shape on the screen and a three-dimensional form in our minds. This is why we often talk about a character's silhouette. If you fill a character's image in with a solid black, you will see only its shape, its silhouette. We should design our character, its pose, and its placement within the composition considering its two-dimensional interpretation.

Light and Patterns

Light patterns provide a way for an artist to break through the object contours and arrange the best shapes for telling a story. Any picture can be thought of as a puzzle pattern of two-dimensional shapes. There are dark, light, and various colored shapes. The shapes of negative space between objects also form part of the puzzle. Sometimes the shapes of the darks and lights do not reveal an object's contours but cut across the contours and background to create different shapes and new design possibilities. A strong light may place the shaded side of a character's face into black shadow. If the background is also black, then the head will merge with the background and some of the outside edge will be lost. The outer contour of the character's head will be less apparent than the light pattern on the face. Light and shadow patterns can create varied shapes regardless of the original contours of the objects. Filmmakers, photographers, and artists of all kinds have realized that lighting can redesign your world and create many compositional choices and dramatic possibilities.

Contrast

Visual contrast means that one thing in the image looks different from everything else. It may be the one window light that is on in a big house with many windows, a small red fish swimming in a school of blue and gray fish. It may be the one person who gets up and leaves in an auditorium of seated, stationary people. Our eyes are drawn to things that stand out against the sameness of their surroundings. You can direct the viewer's eye by making something stand out visually. It is always important to consider where you want your audience to be focused in any shot. Don't give the audience too many things to focus on or they may not see what you need them to see. *Upstaging* is a term used to suggest that the wrong thing is stealing the attention away from where it is supposed to be. Don't let the wrong thing upstage your main area of focus. There should be one idea per storyboard and one main thing to focus the audience's attention on in each shot.

Camera Focus

The depth of field in a camera has been used to "blur out" the background, while the foreground is in focus and then to reverse the effect and let the foreground become out of focus, while the background becomes clear. This is called *rack focus* and represents a way that the live-action camera operator keeps the audience looking at the right thing.

Rack Focus

Contrast of Scale

One way to think about scale is the distance of the main subject from the viewer. The distance of the subject is determined by the distance of the camera from the subject or the way the zoom is set on the lens. The standard categories are close-up, mid-shot, and long shot. There are also extreme close-up, medium long shot, and other intermediate variations. Of course, close-up shots are more intimate and can show the audience subtleties of facial expression or beads of sweat on someone's upper lip. Distance shots can make the character look small and vulnerable in the environment.

Close-up, medium shot, long shot, Storyboards by Steve Gordon

Many beginners tend to keep their camera at the same distance from the subject throughout a scene. You should use a range of shots to give your film visual variety and to take advantage of the emotional or psychological message that each type of shot can convey. You may want to avoid a medium-to-medium shot unless you change camera angle. It is often better to use a medium to close-up shot if the angle stays the same.

Another aspect of scale relates to the comparative size of one shape or area of the screen to another shape or area. Since we are attracted to visual contrast, we tend to notice the shape that is biggest. In a cowboy movie gunfight, the camera may be behind one cowboy's holstered gun as his hand twitches in anticipation. This silhouette may fill 80% of the screen, making his opponent look small and distant. This kind of shot is surely more dynamic than simply filming the entire gunfight in profile with the camera the same distance from each cowboy. Compose your shots with consideration to a variety of shape sizes. The visual richness that shape size variation brings to your shots can translate into a more powerful telling of your story.

Pictorial Space

There is a great scene in the live-action film *The Abyss* 1989, twentieth Century Fox. The screen is shown as if we are looking through the side of an aquarium. The aquarium is filling with water and our human character is drowning. The camera keeps moving closer, the water keeps rising, and the ceiling keeps dropping until there is only a narrow strip of air space. Our character struggles to push her mouth into the narrow airspace to stay alive. The audience is watching, often with their necks fully extended and their chins pushing up, as they feel the space filling up and the anguished character fighting for her last breath. This is a great example of how the director makes the audience feel and on some levels experience the anguish of drowning through the manipulation of pictorial space.

Drowning Scene from the film Abyss

The way we use the actual, 2D space of the screen and the illusion of 3D space that our film characters move in are each distinctly significant elements of staging. A character may be staged to look open and free or trapped and claustrophobic. A feeling of submission or dominance can be attained if one character is up looking down at another character who is down looking up. A tracking shot could have the camera follow a character walking to the right but the character is on the right side of the screen. This draws attention to the space behind him and may suggest he is being followed. If this same scene has the character on the left, we may feel that he has a comfortable amount of space for the character to move forward into, so we may simply feel that he is moving merrily along his way. There are many ways to change the staging and, as a result, change the story.

Character has space to move into

Nose Room

If a character looks to the right and speaks to someone, you may want to put the character on the left third of the composition so she has some room to look and speak into on the screen. When you show who she is speaking to, you may want to put that person on the left third for the same reason. You can keep the space feeling fluid and dynamic by considering the attraction of the empty space around the subject.

Character is possibly being followed

Shallow, Flat, Deep, and Ambiguous Space

A scene that takes place in a small room with the back wall parallel to the screen could be considered a flat, shallow space. Another shot may follow a character as he disappears down a long hallway revealing a deeper space. A film that runs for 30 minutes in a shallow space may suddenly change, transporting the viewer to the top of a mountain overlooking a vast panoramic landscape. This contrast may cause a very strong emotional reaction in the viewer. The restriction of shallow space may reinforce an idea of limitation and entrapment while deep space may suggest the opposite effect. The contrast of one to the other can strengthen the impact of each. Your story may require the depiction of a world from a bug's point of view or through the eyes of an eagle. Sometimes the story requires that the audience be kept uncomfortable or unsure about the space. Dreams and memories may be more effective if we are not entirely grounded in a familiar space. Other kinds of poetic solutions may require a more surreal departure from common experience of space. A film can make the audience feel the sensation of a type of space and the psychological associations that come with that experience. Good staging will require a careful consideration of the type of space a shot is using in order to put the audience in the right emotional state.

Research

There is one sure way to learn and explore staging possibilities, and that is to study the choices of other filmmakers. Watch a film and notice the filmmaker's staging decisions. Watch for the lighting and placement of important information and ask yourself, "How did the filmmaker get me to see what I needed to see?" Think about how the filmmaker may have considered the emotional aspects of the story when making staging decisions. Most importantly, make drawings of what you see. Simple thumbnails showing placement and tonal distribution can help you understand how grandeur and intimacy or pathos and comedy can be presented to an audience in the best way. Learn how the masters achieve that magical experience we all recognize when we are truly moved by a great film.

Studies of Staging from Akira Kurosawa's "Ran" by storyboard artist Paul Briggs

Storyboarding Checklist

How do you know if your storyboards are doing everything they need to do to captivate and inform your audience? We are often trying to consider many issues at once when planning a film. This checklist may prevent you from missing important choices.

- What is the important storytelling information in this frame? What exactly needs to be seen?

- Does the image convey the emotion of story as well as the specific data of the narrative?

- Does the image tell what is happening clearly? Is my craftsmanship effective? Is there any chance the audience could be confused or unsure about what they are seeing?

- Are there "gaps" in my storyboard? Do I need more panels to make the story complete and to keep the flow of action and ideas working?

- Will the viewers look where I want them to look? Have I chosen the best camera angle? Do I need lighting or color to direct the audience's eye?

- Is this panel too predictable? Do I need to spice things up? What are some other options?

- Should I consider putting foreground elements between the camera and the main subject of my shot? Should I use frame in frame for this composition?

- Do the drawings flow visually and stylistically from the panels before and after?

- Should I move the camera to change this shot from the shot before and after, where and why?

- Have I put the audience in the action by using POV and other more intimate shots or have I kept the audience observing at a distance? Which is more appropriate at this point in the story?

- Will the storyboards that I am doing now require that I go back and re-evaluate and then redraw some of my earlier story panels?

- Have I captured the most telling pose, gesture, action, or facial expression? Does the body language convey what my character is thinking, feeling, or doing? Do I need more reference, research?

- Does the character appear to be moving, in action, when action is required or does it look like a frozen pose? Do I need speed lines, arrows, or multiple images? Can I represent the essence or totality of this action in one drawing, or will I need to break it down into several panels?

- Are the light and atmosphere important parts of telling my story, setting its mood or emotional climate?

- What kind of space is right for this scene: flat, shallow, deep, ambiguous? Which best reinforces this aspect of the story? Is it important that my audience know of the season, time of day, or weather conditions?
- Have I shown my boards to other people for a fresh perspective?

Summary

- Staging refers to the way you show us things in a film.
- The design of the shot can direct the audience to see what you want them to see.
- The frame shape is your first design element.
- Some subdivisions of the frame are more effective than others.
- You can re-design the composition with lighting and framing devices.
- Contrast of movement, color, tonal value, scale, and texture can direct the eye.
- Illusionistic space in a shot and the two-dimensional space of the screen can both be manipulated for emotional effect.
- The empty space around things helps to tell the story.
- Learn good staging by studying good filmmakers.

Recommended Readings

1. Marlie Begleiter, *From Word to Image Storyboarding and the Filmmaking Process.*
2. Nancy Beiman, *Prepare to Board.*
3. Bruce Block, *The Visual Story.*
4. Mark T. Byrne, *Animation—The Art of Layout.*
5. Jeremy Vineyard, *Setting Up Your Shots.*

Appendix A

What's on the DVD

Industry Animations		Student Animations		Beginning Acting: A Demonstration	Industry Interviews
Gopher Broke	2D Animatic	The Animator and the Seat	Process	Psychophysical Gesture	Paul Briggs
The ChubbChubbs		Caps		Scene Work	Jim Story
Early Bloomer 4:50		Catch		Iconic Moments	Steve Gordon Storyboards
		The Dancing Thief	2D Animatic	Tomatoes	Barry Cook
		Das Floss	Making of	Closing: Kate Alexander	Frank Gladstone
		Fantasia Taurina			Kathy Altieri
		Eureka!	Process		Kendal Cronkhite
		My Great Big Robot from Outer Space Ate My Homework	Process		
		The Kite	Process		
		Kuhfo			
		Noggin	Process		
		Our Special Day	2D Animatic		
		Poor Bogo			
		Respire, Mon Ami	2D Animatic		
		Ritterschlag	Making of		
		Maria Clapsis	Storyboards and Animatics		

Process Menu Breakdowns:

1. **The Animator and the Seat**
   a. 2D Animatic
   b. Character and Environment Designs

2. **Eureka!**
   a. Storyboards
   b. Beat Boards
   c. 3D Model Facial Tests

3. **A Great Big Robot From Outer Space Ate My Homework**
   a. 2D Animatic
   b. Acting Reference
   c. Character and Environment Designs

4. **The Kite**
   a. 2D Animatic
   b. Character and Environment Designs

5. **Noggin**
   a. Character and Environment Designs

6. **Maria Clapsis Storyboards and Animatics**
   a. Giraffe Storyboard
   b. Pirate Character Designs, Environment Designs, Thumbnails, Storyboards
   c. AIDS Animatic
   d. I Saw a Ship Animatic
   e. Jack and Jill Animatic
   f. Knave of Hearts Animatic

Glossary

A

Accumulated Conflicts—multiple problems build in number or complexity through different and unrelated events, a way for conflict to progress.

Acting Is "Truth"—authenticity of action and feeling; conveying real emotion that is specific to the moment the actor is playing.

Actions—the physical choices the character uses in concert with the intentions.

Adrenaline Moment—something that happens to a character that is of such great emotional significance that he will remember it when he is 90.

Animatic—a video or digital film made of storyboard drawings sometimes with sound for preview and pacing purposes.

Appeal—the aspect of the character's design or personality that makes us want to know more about her and makes us empathize with her plight.

Arc—the physical, psychological, spiritual, or emotional change the main character experiences between the beginning and end of the story.

Archetype—a pervasive idea or image that serves as an original model from which copies are made. In film, this translates to base-line characters that appear in nearly all feature films: the hero, the mentor, the shadow, the herald, the trickster, the threshold guardian, and the shapeshifter.

Aspect Ratio—the proportion of the height to the width of the film image frame.

Attribute—a quality or characteristic of a person, thing, group, character, and so on.

B

Beat Sheet—a written description of the events and images that make up each change in a scene.

Boom—a long pole that holds a camera or a microphone up above the action being recorded as the boom operator is off to the side and out of the scene. A shot that moves the camera in a vertical direction.

Brainstorming—a method of problem solving that involves the rapid generation of a variety of possible solutions.

Bus-Stop Structure—when an essential secondary character arrives and leaves during parts of the story.

C

Catharsis—the emotional relief felt by the audience at the end of the film.

Character(s)—the personalities that make a story believable. In films, this includes main characters, opposing characters, secondary characters, and extras.

Character Profile—the history and attributes that form the personality of the character.

Cinematography—the photographic aspects of filmmaking. The field of study about film and filmmaking.

Circular Structure—stories where the characters wind up when they begin.

Cliché—an idea that has lost its originality and become trite from overuse.

Climax—when the main character is in direct conflict with the obstacle.

Collage—an image or artwork that is made up of a number of separate images such as photographs or pieces of paper.

Compounded Conflict—a single problem builds in layers upon itself through similar or related events. A way for conflict to progress.

Concept—the underlying larger idea that the animation communicates. The deeper meaning of the story.

Condensation—a strategy to find a way to simplify a story for animation by combining or condensing one or more ideas.

Conflict—conflict is the problem that keeps the character from reaching his or her goal. There are three forms of conflict: character vs. character, character vs. environment, and character vs. self.

Continuity—a term that refers to the natural, meaningful progression from one shot to the next relative to time, space, lighting, details, and so on.

Crane—a machine that lifts the camera and camera operator up and down often as the camera is recording.

D

Depth of Field—property of a camera lens that determines how deep the camera will see things in focus.

Dialogue—the lines spoken by a character in a film.

Displacement—to change the point of view or context of the story while maintaining the same story.

Dolly (or Truck)—a device for a camera to be placed on so it can be rolled forward and backward while the camera is recording. The corresponding shot may also be called a dolly or truck shot.

E

Editing—the process of physically or digitally putting the shots and transitions in order as well as the changing and arranging of all other aspects of a film. The term is used often to connote cutting things out of a film or story.

Emotional Recall—one element of the psychological mind; drawing on your own memories and experience to generate emotion.

Empathy—one element of the psychological mind; actors imagine and "feel" themselves in a specific situation to generate emotion. Also called the magic "If."

Ending (also called *Resolution*)—what the viewer needs to bring emotional relief and answer all of the questions of the story. The ending must transform the audience or character.

Establishing Shot—an opening shot, often a long shot, which shows the building, location, or other place where the action will be happening.

Ethics—the values and morals that guide the decisions of an individual.

External Monologue—what the audience thinks or feels at each beat in the story.

Exposition—the main character and location are introduced.

G

Gesture—the use of movement to express thought or emotion.

Goal—this is the physical object the character wants to obtain: the princess, the treasure, the girl, the boon, the bounty, the recognition, and so on.

Graphic Mass—a term that refers to the amount of screen area occupied by a shape or object in a film.

H

Hard Light—a bright light that casts dark shadows.

Herald—the character that announces the call to adventure and delivers other important information throughout the story.

Hero—the character through which the story is told.

High Key Lighting—bright light sources that cast light shadows.

I

Inciting Incident—an unexpected event that throws the main character into action and pursuit of a goal.

Iconic Moment—the important storytelling images in the scene.

Image—a thought that gives the actor the ability to access a picture in his or her mind that will create emotion.

Improvisation—unscripted, uninhibited play to discover something new.

Inciting Moment—the unexpected event that begins the story.

Internal Monologue—what a character thinks or feels at each beat in the story.

L

Lens Flare—the effect of a circle or other pattern of light seen on a film when the camera lens is pointed directly at the sun or some other light source.

Live Action—a film term that refers to the use of human actors.

Local Color (Local Values)—the actual color of something without regard to the amount or quality of the light that is falling on it.

Location—the environment, place, time period, and/or atmosphere that supports the story.

Low Key Lighting—minimal light sources that cast deep shadows, creating a scene that is very dark.

M

Mask/Shell—a composite of personality traits through which a character's emotions are filtered.

Mask Shot—a cutout, stencil shape that masks the image so it looks like it is being seen through a keyhole or binoculars.

Monomyth—what Joseph Campbell called the story that appears across all cultures that involves universal images and characters.

Mentor—the ally who helps the hero.

Metaphor—something used, a symbol or replacement, to represent something else.

Montage—a collection of shots or images that are presented in a sequence in a film that collectively create meaning. Often more than one image can be seen at a time. These could be still images and may be in any order.

Motion Blur—the blur created on individual movie frames when the camera films things that are moving fast or when the camera itself is moving fast.

N

Narration—the use of a third-party voiceover to tell a story.

Need—in order for the story to have meaning for the character, he or she needs to learn something to achieve his or her goal.

O

Objective/Goal—what a character wants.

Over the Shoulder Shot—A shot from a camera that is placed behind and above the shoulder of a character so the audience will see what that character sees.

P

Pan—a camera move across a scene usually from a single position by pivoting.

Parallel Structure—when more than one event is taking place. These events, in most cases, eventually converge.

Physical Gesture—the psychological or emotional truth that is revealed in the physicality of an actor's body movement.

Ping Pong—a story format where the character moves back and forth between similar but escalating obstacles and similar attempts at resolution.

Plot—the sequence of events in a story, including the emotional motivations of the characters to move the audience through the story. Plot must be whole. It must have a beginning, middle, and end.

Point of View—the outlook or position of the character in relationship to the story.

Premise—a basic overview of the plot of a story. It is usually no more than a few sentences that introduce the main character, main conflict, and an emotional tag that motivate the audiences to watch the film.

Process Boards—storyboards developed for one's own planning of a film, not meant to be presented to others.

Prop—a physical object—tables, pictures, plants, buildings, bridges, tools, weapons, etc.— that populate a scene and are used by the character to support the story.

Presentation Boards—storyboards that are cleaned up and made attractive to be presented to others.

Psychological Mind—the emotional life of a character that is developed using either emotional recall or empathy.

Psycho-Physical Action—a theory developed by Constantin Stanislavski in the 20th century that helps an actor access the human emotional core; utilizes both the psychological mind and physical gesture to generate emotion.

R

Reaction Shots—a shot that shows the facial expression or performance of a character as the character responds to something it has seen or experienced.

Resolution—the point in the story where the main character succeeds or fails in such a way that the character arcs and the audience experiences relief or catharsis. The end.

Reverse Shot—a shot that reverses the direction of the camera from the previous shot.

Rising Conflict—someone or something gets between the main character and the goal, making the conflict worse. This is usually done in two to three events.

S

Scratch Track—a substitute or stand-in soundtrack for a film or animatic.

Scrolling—an editing transition which has one shot appear to slide in from off screen and cover or push the previous shot out.

Shadow—the villain or major protagonist.

Shapeshifter—this character is not who she appears or who she presents herself to be.

Shot—an image that is created in a film from the time the camera starts recording until it is shut off. In editing it is the images seen from one cut to the next.

Soft Light—lower contrast lighting with soft shadows.

Shot List—a written description of each camera angle and camera move for each shot.

Show, Don't Tell—this is the concept that, in film, you cannot tell what a character is thinking. Instead of using voice-over, dialogue, or written signage, make sure you communicate everything through visual cues and actions.

Space—the empty area in a set or stage where the action takes place.

Speed Lines—lines trailing objects that are drawn to make the objects or characters appear as if they are moving and leaving behind a blur or a trail of wind.

Status—the power a character wields in a relationship or negotiation with another character.

Story—a character's experience through a conflict. A story has a character who wants something badly and is having trouble getting it.

Storyboard—a visual blueprint of the animation that shows the staging of the camera and the strong pose of the character that *should* be produced in the film.

Story Question—the inciting moment sets up questions in the mind of the audience that must be answered by the end of the story.

Subtext—when a character says one thing but means another.

T

Texture—the tactile surface quality of an object.

Theme—the underlying larger idea that the animation communicates. The deeper meaning of the story.

Threshold Guardian—a character or object that the character must get past to proceed on a quest.

Thumbnail Drawings—small, rough drawings made to plan an image or sequence of images.

Track—cameras were actually placed on platforms with wheels that rode on small railroad-type tracks to move and follow a character's action. Any shot that has the camera staying with a character or object as it moves in a scene.

Trickster—this character is usually the comic relief in the story, sometimes leading the hero off-track or away from the goal.

Z

Zooms—a shot that uses camera lens magnification to bring the image close or push it back.

Index